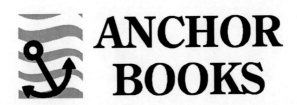

ANCHOR BOOKS

AS THE NIGHTS DRAW IN

Edited by

Sarah Marshall

First published in Great Britain in 2005 by
ANCHOR BOOKS
Remus House,
Coltsfoot Drive,
Peterborough, PE2 9JX
Telephone (01733) 898102

SB ISBN 1 84418 391 2

FOREWORD

Anchor Books is a small press, established in 1992, with the aim of promoting readable poetry to as wide an audience as possible.

We hope to establish an outlet for writers of poetry who may have struggled to see their work in print.

The poems presented here have been selected from many entries, and as always editing proved to be a difficult task.

I trust this selection will delight and please the authors and all those who enjoy reading poetry.

Sarah Marshall
Editor

CONTENTS

THE BEAUTY OF AUTUMN

Autumn follows summer, which paints a lovely scene,
The changing colours of the leaves, with colours so serene.
Leaves change from brown to golden, from russet then to red,
Just like an artist's painting - what more can there be said?
As autumn months progress, the leaves begin to fall,
Carpeting the shady woods, they fall on ground and wall.
Walks amongst the crispy leaves, their colours now are fading,
The bareness of these lovely trees shows winter now is trading.
The evening air is cooler, the nights are getting short,
But still these months are beautiful, such beauty can't be bought.
As autumn follows summer, the swallows sing their song,
Preparing for their journey they line up in a throng.
Flying to some distant shore, some far and distant place,
They will return, now they must fly, with dignity and grace.
Autumn months are beautiful, though cooler than of spring,
The glory of this perfect month, its peace will always bring.

Winter follows autumn, the weather's damp and cold,
Yet still it holds a mystic charm, its pleasure to unfold,
The temperatures are plummeting, we struggle to keep warm,
We sit around a log-filled fire and watch the flames that form,
Outside the world is sleeping, the mountains capped with ice,
They stand in wondrous beauty, gripped in the winter's vice,
The snowdrops are protected from a blanket made of snow,
Protected from the frost and cold, they nurture strength to grow.
Streams are frozen solid, no birds sing in the trees,
No flowers in abundance, no warm or sultry breeze,
No chirping of the crickets, no croaking of the frogs,
No sounds of lambs a-bleating, no sound of barking dogs,
Though summer days are over and birds now seldom sing.
We'll smile through frozen winter and look toward the spring,
When we see the snowdrops, we'll know that spring is near,
The circle has completed the seasons of the years.

Marjorie J Picton

AUTUMN

Leaves, like confetti, tumbling down,
A breeze gently blowing them along the ground,
Settling on gardens and clogging up drains,
Getting very slippery and brown when it rains,
Trees looking barer by the day,
With just a few leaves that won't blow away,
Crunching like corn flakes when curled and dry,
Swirling in corners, they catch the eye.

The colour of deep burnt orange is there,
The low glow of the sun, with no warmth to spare,
A cat under a bush avoiding the showers,
Wanting to curl near a fire for hours and hours,
The birds that are left are bedraggled and wet,
Their singing has ceased . . . now the robin we'll get,
His red breast a treat on the dull autumn days,
Finding its food as it goes on its way.

Flowers shrivel up and call it a day,
Thick jumpers come out, T-shirts put away,
Drawing the curtains earlier each night,
Barbecues in sheds, now warmth is firelight,
The moon up high looking misty and wet,
Autumn's here, so that's as good as it gets,
Only brave animals will venture outside,
But us, being humans, just stay home and hide.

Elsie Kemp

OCTOBER RAIN

Hissing rain beats,
dampens leaves
landing;
their yearly fall
a hallowed ceremony.

Forsaken trees stand,
barren branches
everlasting
beholder to pools
of languid
water.

Children swiftly jump,
pitter-patter,
puddles
creating a mirror
of cherished
memories.

An autumnal downpour
woven into
soil.
Sky and plants
are eternally
cleansed.

Julius Howard

ANCIENT PLACES

Lost in a clearing,
the river making waves out
of the trees . . .
pieces of sky suddenly appear
blue in-between the high branches . . .
they catch the light,
holding it safe for the day . . .
but I can see night gathering
its forces,
shadows romping in the
corners of scrub and bush,
tangled like hair full of thorns,
touching my skin, leaving lines
of blood where nature claims
its right to hold sway within
the forest . . .

I'm moving ahead of the day,
with the night a furtive beast
grasping every shadow,
clinging to the last of the
moonbeams playing mystery
inside this cathedral bowery . . .
there is music in the air,
water sounds rippling in melody
with the bees and the ancient
whispers still haunting this
quiet sanctuary from the frantic
world screaming beyond
the river bank . . .

Walking back towards
the road I leave glory behind,
hoping it will still be there
when I return . . .

Peter J Maher

AUTUMN DREAMS

There's a cool edge to the air this time of year.

The day's core's still warm
but we want more of the broad, bright
and balmy summer days and nights
before the switch was flicked
between August's exuberant heat
and September's temperance.

More - of the sun-washed dawns when we know
before curtains are drawn that there is
definite promise of a light-filled day,
a peach sunset and a velvet, starlit night.

More - of the grass-green smell
of repose on a rug on the lawn
of feeling happy to be born
when walking with a back that's warm as a lover's hug.

More - of the late evening light
so convenient that we might continue reading or gardening
into the early hours of night, then only finally closing the door
on the day's warmth stored in the soil.

Before the coming of the biting cold
when vibrant green turns gold
there is this brief moment
of longing
in earliest autumn -
before we allow ourselves
to be charmed into a new season
and relax into
her own warm pleasures.

Maureen Horne

ROLLING THROUGH THE SEASONS

I can now feel the chill of a morning
as I gingerly step out of my bed
the trees are shedding their leaves
autumnal colours, browns, yellows and reds.

As I stand and admire the rich tapestry
of changing seasons with differing hues
nature fills me with wonder and appreciation
that's Mother Earth to me and you.

As the days move on and the wind starts to howl
the leaves are plucked and blown from the trees
tumbling and twirling, they fall to the floor
where they dry out and wither with ease.

To go for a walk and stroll through the park
with the dead leaves crunching under my feet
wrapped up in my warm winter woollies
recycling my own body heat.

Young children with rosy glowing faces,
running and kicking the leaves as they go
hunching up as the wind blows away cobwebs
this is the autumn we have all come to know.

The summer has gone and autumn is here
the birds heading due south for the winter
daylight hours drawing short with darkening skies
summer days seem too far off to ponder.

Margaret M Donnelly

AUTUMNAL SPLENDOUR

This is the time for colder winds
Night-time frosts and morning mists
But a sunny day can still be warm
It invites you out so don't resist.

This is the time for falling leaves
Like golden snowflakes they flutter down
Windswept piles of crispy colours
Form a carpet on the ground.

This is the time for stormy skies
A mixture of grey and blue
But if you're really lucky
Then you'll see some rainbows too.

This is the time for spiders' webs
With silken gossamer threads
You don't see them and walk through them
Their clinging strands around your head.

This is the time for beautiful sunsets
Red-gold colours in the sky
A stunning backdrop for migrating birds
As to warmer climes they fly.

This is the time for warming fires
And as the shadows softly creep
In all her autumnal splendour
Mother Nature sighs and goes to sleep.

Carolyn Jones

AUTUMNAL ADVERSITY

Crimson-coated leaves clinging
to trees which Nature nurtures
as they struggle for survival
throughout the coming winter months.

The cruel wind carries them off
to an unknown destination,
as the air howls derisively
at this display of destruction.

The sun, conspicuous by its absence,
sits in the shadows, waiting
whilst Mr Hyde is hard at work
doing his worst.

Paul Burton

REFLECTION

Still the sun shines but the warmth is gone
Autumn resides
Her dark evenings enfold us.
The wind has an edge to its lifting appeal
Drawing tarnished leaves to carpet the baked earth.
Flowers wither, reabsorbing their life essence
Gathering strength to lie dormant until spring
When new life will burst forth.
For now we will shelter
Draw the curtains, keep warm
And put pen to paper
The time for reflection is here.

Karen Davies

AUTUMN'S CLOCK

Bracken burns the forest floor
The auburn leaves are falling,
Summer's closing all its doors
And autumn's clock is primed and calling.
Howling wind and thrashing rain
Attack all coastal sea defences,
It's a long, long way from scorching days
And a shock to all our senses.
But it has charm,
This changing season
There's a crispness to the air,
The colours on the trees are blazing
There's busy creatures everywhere.
They know that every day's a race
And now's the time to hoard and store,
Once autumn's gone and winter's here
The forest floor will start to snore.

Andrew Hobbs

AUTUMN COLOURS

Trees in all their autumn glory
Covered in heatless flame.
Proclaiming the winter story
Gone are the greens of summer now
Gold, red and brown on every bough.
Leaves fall silent to the forest floor
Making the squirrel hide his winter store.
The sun flickers through this golden hue
Reflecting past beauty.

Pamela Gormley

AUTUMN BLESSINGS

Autumnal colours of red and gold
Upon the hedges and deciduous trees,
Berries ripened to a rich crimson red
Attracting the birds before winter's freeze.

Shuffling through leaves, a childhood pleasure,
An abundance of acorns, the squirrels' delight,
Children collect conkers, fun without measure,
To a warmer climate the swallows take flight.

Chestnuts and walnuts fall to the ground,
Fruits of the orchards ready to reap,
Sloes and blackberries make fine home-made wine,
Hedgehogs prepare for their winter sleep.

We attend the harvest festival
To give our thanks and pray,
In recognition of our blessings
Which we appreciate every day.

D Kowalska

AUTUMN RAIN

Raindrops freckling
on a city centre puddle,
shivering outwards:
a kaleidoscope of
dimpling circles.

A slow motion circle explodes
with tremulous effect,
winnowing its way
to murky edges
of early morning darkness.

Sarah Nichols

AUTUMN DAYS

Skies, cloud scudded,
Above trees, whose yellow leaves
Hang trembling until,
Ruffled by wind fingers,
They spiral gently down.

Now winds, briskly blowing
Across cloud tossed skies,
Waft yellow, brittle leaves,
Rustling them into crisp heaps
Which blackbirds busily scatter.

Bare branches; silhouettes
Against pale lemon skies.
The last crumpled leaves
Swirl, to lie silent
In wet lank grass.

Audrey Roberts

THE FALL

Cruel winds curse
The forest deep
Defrocked
Ashamed
Trees weep
Rain splatters
Branches
Scratch the sky
A sombre mulch
Of autumn wreaths
Lay prostrate
On the ground.

Joyce Graham

AUTUMN

The brilliance of daylight becomes rich in colour
The sunshine has gone now but no need for dolour

The vegetation accepts ageing with such dignity
And autumnal beauty abounds through every forest,
field and lea

Copper, rust and gold, amidst the greeny-brown
All is wrinkled and withered, as the growth slows down

Little hiding creatures and camouflaged, speckled birds
Crispy leaves to stamp upon, there's no suitably
expressive words.

All those stale, dead leaves and naked trees
Getting ready, bark and body for the *big freeze*

Leaf after leaf, decks the ground
Like a carpet protecting all around

All is open and bare, where do all the leaves go?
It's all almost over now - the finale of the snow

The seasons are like slabs of cake, divided by a knife
It's almost as if this process proves that there is an afterlife

Take a tree, how can its leaves die one day then suddenly revive?
This is magical and mystical, Lord, it's so good to be alive

Sirocco cloudy days and peeking rays of sunshine
Through crumpled, crunchy woods, the trunks stand in line

Like an army of soldiers, their bows salute the brave
and weathered earth
This is the calm before the storm - and then it's - the rebirth

The last flies of summer starting to die
As the dark nights start invading the sky

The end is near now, the wise all agree
That Nature reclaims all of us - eventually.

Lynn Paston

WE COME AND GO!

Natural, genetic, homogeneous, ephemeral
Who knows what is what and is correctly defined
The scientists describe disease as abnormal
But moral values know no confines.

The role for family, heads or tails
Mothers at work, not to earn a crust
Send children to school, fathers to gaols
Put a roof over their head or end up as dust.

Never-ending debates and quarrels
Bankers, loan sharks, your mother or the one you marry
Who pays for this, tax earners, they have us over a barrel
Whether King or Pope, Lord Mayor or clerk, time does not tarry.

If the planet could, on the stock market, float
Not keep revolving, like a pendulum standing
Could we afford it, even have a stake in an infinitesimal valued note
Because some big wig devalues our contrite, heartfelt panting.

Our hoping for life to bring us more time
Deficiencies replenished like new seasons and harvest
To endure in a state not desperate but sublime
Reflecting on annual seed sowing, smile and be blessed.

Gerasim

AUTUMN

In autumn shadow seeking its reflection
The expression of new season coming in,
This is the real happiness with rich beauty fragrant
The year has come to autumn
And yet nature has made sunshine and shade.

Lingering out the stretches of bracken and gold
To the icy touch of the morning air
Autumn winds are whirling around the meadowlands
Happy with love for the world in my heart,
I can feel the joy of the autumn gold.

October harvest waits for the ploughman's golden hour
Golden of the meadows and blue of the sky,
These are the joys nothing destroys the world.
Tender passion of beautiful golden autumn air
Autumn changes a vision of new season.

Heather Aspinall

STOLEN SUMMER

When dark elastic shadows creep
This Earth that nurtured every blade,
Across a land that yearns for sleep
Beneath October skies betrayed
As autumn strikes with unseen hand,
Each swollen fruit of summer cursed,
Each leaf and bloom that dares to stand,
The season's hands of time reversed
And winter winks a frozen eye
The last of summer's beauty lost
A million stars through blackboard sky
Above a thieving, shameless frost.

Mark L Moulds

SEASON 3

Her language becomes penultimate blizzard
I backfire an hour alone, unescorted
misplacing myself in chilly tree fingers,
the wildwood lacking her summer clothes,
then she leaves, bouncing off flagging skin of bark.

The daylight unenlightened, shadowy night,
insincere afternoon light, stretching bleary eyes
morning slumber becomes a tranquilliser
hibernation in blankets, my captivation,
dragging into a period of wheel turning.

Doddering trees neglect to morning dress,
unbuttoned, bare, too sluggish to be ashamed.
A child, disorientated without the summer haze,
yet, unafraid of this season's change of heart
September's costume ignorant to this October cape.

Luke Kayne

CRAB APPLES AND BLACKBERRIES

Orchard harvest
Pears and plums
Jam pots simmering
Late summer sun.

Blackberries hang
Crab apples fall
Leaves turn gold
September winds.

Song for harvest
Pumpkin pie
Shades of autumn
September moon.

Alison Hitch

SEASONS

With winter knocking on the door
The sequence must have changed
I never noticed autumn
Were the seasons rearranged?
Now what we get we must accept
Unless we go abroad,
At clothing change we are adept
And it's not to be ignored.
I visualise a nice coal fire
Where I look into the flames
These radiators can't compare
Despite their many claims
And as I gaze into my fire
I see a happy 'trog',
who many, many years ago
Sat before a burning log.
In helping to keep families warm
Radiators do their duty,
By comparison to the living fire
They don't qualify for beauty.

Bill Austin

THE SEASONED GARDEN

Summer's end, all is changing,
In the garden set below,
Anticipation and excitement,
My eyes crave the autumn glow,
Eden upon our threshold,
Paradise all at play,
From one season to another,
This is where I'll always stay.

Simon Raymond McCreedy

THE CHANGING SCENE

Some mornings still give out the sun
Autumn's here and well begun
Still some brightly flowers stand
And brave the colder days,
You can feel that winter nip
Creeping in the air,
The laughing wind sends you scurrying
To your cosy fire.

Curtains are drawn early
To keep out the evening cold
The dark nights are upon us
Spreading shadows all unfold,
Warming soups and hot buttered toast
Is on the menu now
Hands clasped round a hot, milky drink
A comfort at bedtime,
Trees have nearly lost all their leaves by now
Branches look like skeletons hanging on the boughs.

Away go summer dresses, shorts and T-shirts too
Sandals, pumps and flip-flops join the summer crew
Put away till next year with the other trendy gear.

Different shades of golden browns and yellows too
That's the autumn colours, a change that is all new,
Through the night the wind has worked
To create a wonderful sight
A golden carpet at your feet,
Your very own autumn scene.

Mary Neill

AUTUMN

Everybody knows what autumn is about.
Getting rid of the old, making way for the new.
Making sure that everything is done,
so that you don't have to lift a finger until Christmas time arrives.
But very few realise the true beauty behind this cold and rainy season.
Just look around you and you'll see squirrels going from tree to tree,
stacking up food for the winter, and there it is in the trees.
The leaves of red and yellow in different shades,
the few remains of a forgotten day
that tries to hang on for as long as possible.
Sadly that's not long enough, if I walk by tomorrow,
it will probably lie in the grass waiting for the wind to send it
twirling to whereabouts unknown, but it stays put for now.
As I walk around I hear a chirping sound.
Looking around I see a small bird resting in a maple tree.
Having the possibility to enjoy nature taking its course is a rare gift.
The runnel between the two oak trees is seemingly covered with leaves,
how any fish could ever survive there is beyond my knowledge.
As all of this goes on, one must ask him or herself,
have I chosen the correct way of living,
or am I bound to fall like the leaves off the tree?
As I walk through town I notice how quiet it is.
Barely a footstep is heard.
I guess most people stay inside these cold days.
I don't fathom why, it might be cold
but the sun shines brighter than ever before
and even though my eyes water from the gusts of wind,
I just sit back relaxing and letting the wind take my senses
to warmer places.
It's getting darker by the hour and the cold winds embrace me.

Lars Petter Wellbring

GLIMPSES OF AUTUMN

The first signs of autumn are at hand
Tortoise comes home to hibernate
Even his thick shell cannot withstand
Winter's intemperate
Away from his native land
Slow moving and ponderous
He burrows under fallen beech masts
Ancient, prehistoric, wondrous
He sleeps and fasts
Until spring

The trees drop their loads
Horse chestnuts thump down to ground
Spilling over paths and roads
Waiting to be found
By little boys
A roseate glow down-lights forest features
Illuminating fly agarics and shaggy ink-caps
Where are those elfin creatures?
Whimsical, androgynous, mishaps
Created in folklore

Does the clock spring forward?
Or should it now fall back
I, like many others, very soon lose track
Autumn segues into winter weather
Leaves are covered by a patina of snow
Bare branches, holly berries and wind resistant heather
This is when we really know
Winter has arrived

Eric Jackson

AUTUMN

The pleasant sunshine's all around, skies are blue and clear,
The leaves are turning into gold, autumn is now near.

Blackberries in the hedgerow on the path to town,
The golden gleam from gorse mound, the distant hill to crown.

All is fair as Nature waits for her winter sleep,
No time is so beautiful, why will people weep?

Because summer is over and spring has long gone,
Even autumn's passed for me and winter has yet to come . . .

But I still enjoy the beauty of one more autumn fair,
Enjoy the lovely colour and the cool, clear air.

And when at last long winter comes, I just hope and pray,
That I may see another spring, summer and autumn gay.

Clifford E Growcott

AUTUMN MEANS WINTER

It's the time of year when the sun begins to turn down,
The leaves start turning, they fall then they're blown.

Each day is shorter, each night a little long,
Quite soon at midnight we'll hear the midday bird song.

The evenings are cooler, the mornings quite chill,
It won't be long before the temperature's at nil.

I used to get depressed at autumnal time of year,
Not because I don't like the fall, but because winter is getting near.

But I have learnt a way from all my hibernating fear
Is to find a new job each autumn in the other hemisphere.

Alan Bruce Thompson

THE BROWN TIME

The time has come, a comforting,
When warm jackets and collars turned,
To snuggle up your ears and neck to autumn's biting turns.
The leaves begin to brown and fall from resplendent green,
The birds sound so melancholy wishing for a dream.
The grass is littered, crunching with leaves upon the ground
And bared branches sleepily sway, soon to rest, winding down
And people walk more slowly, as if enjoying change,
A sign that summer's over, a gradual, gradual thing.
Admiring the sunset and long shadows on the ground,
To each of us a mystery, a time to wonder on what has passed.
But autumn flows bring order to a rested mind.

Robin Quest

OCTOBER

Rosehips, rain-glossed, gleam
from darkening hedgerows
as leaves die back and wither;
but the ivy thrives.
Deep red haws tempt the
field mouse and the sparrow
from safe cover,
rowanberries shout in bright
abundance, 'Here we are.'
The wind, hearing, shakes them down.
Blood-red spots on grass and paving
foretell a killing winter.

Betty Norton

TOMATOES HAVE SHOT UP IN PRICE

Tomatoes have shot up in price,
Which, on the surface, is not very nice;
But think what this means -
Cabbages and beans,
Squashes and sweet pumpkin pies!

Yes, we are now in September,
And now is the time to remember
The great deal of worth
Of things that grow under the earth;
There is something for each family member.

New potatoes or yam
And onion to go with roast lamb;
Turnip, parsnip and swede
Give us the goodness we need,
While blackberries make a nice jam.

If the thought of veg makes you mumble
And you're beginning to fidget and fumble,
Before you get flustered,
Just think of hot custard
Poured over a nice apple crumble.

Kathy Rawstron

FRANTIC SEASON

Following the daintiness of spring,
And informality of summer,
Autumn is a strumpet -
Strutting, gaudily dressed,
Dancing a tarantella
Before the death of winter,
Pealing gales of laughter
Tinged with a sob of hysteria.
Wildly strewing garments and possessions
These I will not need
When I fall upon the cooling ground!
Driving the birds and mammals
To ever more energetic hunter gathering.
Fatness of the harvest moon
Mocks at this desperate activity below.
Flashes of gold, flaming to sanguinity,
Frantic season of selfish acquisition
Of food, shelter and warm covering . . .
Until the rapidly falling temperatures
Abruptly strip the world of colour
And still the maelstrom of autumn.

Di Bagshawe

AUTUMN

Autumn: the time leaves change from green
And change to a dazzling multicoloured scene.
Autumn: changing the green of grass,
Now that summer has passed.
Autumn: the time of nature slowing down,
Giving time for animals to change around.
Autumn: the time to change from summer dress,
And into winter's warmest best.
Autumn: the time to skip through fallen leaves,
When no one's looking, if you please.
Autumn: the time for roasted chestnuts
From the hot fire to pluck.
Autumn: the time nature's fruits are gathered in
For different flavours they bring.
Autumn: the time for migrating birds
To move back over wide open seas.
Autumn: the time for evening class
For O and A levels to pass.
Autumn: the time for a good look round,
A good reading book to be found.
Autumn: the time for logs in open grate,
Dashing home, no time to wait.
Autumn: a sip of warm mulled wine
And take a trip back in time.

Robert Gray Sill

As Summer Goes By

The summer months are over
Now that autumn time is here.
No more running through the clover
No more barbecues and beer.

The leaves are changing colour now
There's a chill about the air.
Time to wrap up in our coats
Feel the wind rustle through our hair.

Countryside walks are picturesque
Forever changing scenes.
Many damp and dewy mornings
With cobwebs that just gleam.

The autumn months bring us Hallowe'en
Where ghosts and witches can be seen
Knocking on doors asking, 'Trick or treat?'
I'll give you an apple or a sweet.

Autumn's here and here it's to stay
So make the most of every day.
The weather may be gloomy with not much sun
But look at all that autumn brings
As autumn can be fun.

Cindy Pearse

HARVEST MOON

The longest season of the year
Where matted colours fill the air
Leaves falling, trees dying
Making room for new saplings
Hazy, sleepy afternoons in the sun
Although the days are shorter
The sunshine lasts for much longer
A gentle, cool breeze sweeps across our land
And the ochre scenery melts with the sun
Conkers and chestnuts are soon to be in season
The grass jewelled with dewdrops
Each morning I wake
Birds gathering for their winter nests
A sleepy season holds the harvest
Where children gather in their schools
Singing songs and giving praise
for the year of bountiful food
Conker games in the playground
Is what I remember best
Soaking them in vinegar
Or gluing them like the rest
Warmer colours fill our cheeks
Pink and peach and rouge
Snugly jumpers, those that are too big
A Christmas present from your nan
And all the while approaching winter
As the cool air hardens and the sun fades
Roaring fires light our way
Although sometimes it comes too soon
I like to call it the month of harvest moon.

Barbara Scott

THE GOLDEN SEASON

Autumn is needed
to give earth a rest,
so next summer's fashions
will look at their best.

First are the colours
of leaves' final show:
spectacular beauty
before they let go,

twirling and dancing
and softly drift down,
as chill winds toss trees
and the sky wears a frown.

Mornings are misty
and cobwebs bedewed;
Jack Frost's icy fingers
trace patterns anew.

The air can be foggy
and daylight is short,
we wear extra woollies
and warm fires are sought.

There's beauty in autumn
in red, brown and gold;
a brave final fling
before winter's harsh cold.

Diana Lynch

AUTUMN

With autumn, comes a quiet reflection.
Memories of hot and sunny days.
Nature, just like life, moves on
Prepares us for the parting of the ways.
Gold, brown and red enhance the view,
The smell of bonfires fill the air,
Early morning mists disperse and shining through
We see late flowers sparkling in the morning dew.

Nature is powerful and heartless
And quickly changes from this peaceful theme.
The angry sky grows dark and seems to press
Upon us as we view the scene.
Gale force winds, fallen trees, rivers overflowing
Autumn's temperamental and the storm seems to be growing.

Man's like a cork tossed on the sea, bobbing up and down
Helpless to change the mighty wrath
When nature wears a frown.

Kathleen Holmes

LEAVING

The trap was sprung, a perennial issue.
Death's rank inherent in the raw shot tissue.
Surviving to blossom and then be picked off.
Or, if their colours flew for long enough,
to bask in sun and glory and think they'd won.
But wizened and wasted, their time has come
to join the faceless heap of brown, trodden,
kicked when down, under boots and rotten.
Then after burial or burning, forgotten.

Susannah Pickering

FALLING SMILE

In Sylvan surroundings, autumn's curse
The trees were standing without modesty
Leafage were dropping into tears
All were worn out as memories of pains
Razed away its glamorous verdure
Leaving its slough, standing as a paramour
As an anthropology poser with faded face
Remembering the glory of foregone
The tree shimmering with green in woods
All eyes are turned over around its physique
Can the silence break out?
Remains with ashen face, as an AIDS patient.
To score-out for his sinful lifespan, breathe
Awaiting to arouse a newborn baby with tender leaves.

Bollimuntha Venkata Ramana Rao

AUTUMN

Brown and yellow amidst deep green
It's an autumn scene

Rusting bracken, buzzards high
It's an autumn sky

Winds sigh, chill the bone
It's an autumn moan.

Woodland smells transcend the view
Of the autumn hue

Rustling leaves, birdsong muted
I'm autumn suited.

Frances Oak

ENDLESS AUTUMN

Low morning mist on the field, the icy dew tips your toes
as you walk through the meadows
watching red-blue streamers of swallows depart,
as they fly goodbye for another year.

Nearing the forest where falling leaves dance for you,
every leaf a petal from flower.
Red deer stags roar while squirrels scuffle,
arranging acorns like never before.

Behold colours of a million years, a theatre of complexion -
shades spring and summer never knew
and winter covers with falling snow.
Blushing branches on podium, tempestuous winds are brewing.
For now, the fluttering breeze propels nervous leaves across
earthened ground.

Mid-afternoon sun hallucinates against the perfect clear sky,
as the last of the butterflies flutter and the last of the
hedgehogs hibernate,
ambling their slow, spiky way to the woodpile.

Autumn apples, succulent blackberries,
taste the harvest of fruits that fall.
Sweet potatoes, warm walnuts
and pumpkins from the Hallowe'en ball

Melodious rain spills like joyous tears -
it'll soon be snow, soft to feel.
Surly sky suggests the onset of winter,
hear hushed chirps when you pass by
as feathered birds huddle in the trees that guard.

On an early night, glimpse winter's sight as a sharp cold envelops.
Frost traces the grass as the sun waves goodbye to the sky
the crispness of the air matches each step on the floor.

Some see autumn as a decline in life,
as summer ends, the autumn plans
for a new time, replenishing
and rekindling its senses.
Falling fruits seed new growth.
Autumn is your imagination,
it's an endless autumn for me.

Alex Harford

AUTUMN

Autumn is the time of year
When the air is crisp and fresh
The scenery is pretty
All nice and picturesque

Leaves are changing colour
To yellow, brown and red
Curling up and falling off
To show that they are dead

The weather's turning colder
The evenings drawing in
The wind is getting stronger
Tie down your wheelie bin

Crispy, frosty mornings
The order of the day
Scrape and clean your windscreen
So you can see your way

It's time for wearing sweaters
There's no more summer sun
Winter's coming quickly
Which won't be any fun.

Neil Warren

THE OCTOBER WIND

Falling leaves, swirl and fly;
Racing clouds sweep the sky;
The October wind is howling.

Orange and red leaves, fewer green;
Artists view the changing scene;
The October wind is howling.

Sun weak at misted morn;
Conkers from their branches torn;
The October wind is howling.

Bonfire smoke drifts far away;
Gardeners tidy at end of day;
The October wind is howling.

Witching nights filled with fear;
Winter's frosted breath is near;
The October wind is howling.

Tracey Lynn Birchall

AUTUMN

Sitting here at the window looking out
Or standing looking out . . .
Looking at what you may ask?
The tree that stands there all year round
Tall, slender with your branches out
And to see the flower blooming.
What colour are you going to be?
Light or dark?
What size - big or small?
No one knows.
But you stands there all year round.

Caz Carty

AUTUMN

Summer's over, autumn's here,
Summer clothes put away for another year.
Woollens taken out, another layer worn,
Waiting for another day, a new moon is born.
Evening drawing in, mornings fresh,
Animals prepare for winter, lining their nests.

Leaves changing colour, red, yellow, brown,
Trees shed their leaves, falling on the ground.
Cold, damp mornings, make some feel distressed,
Putting on coats, hats and gloves, we feel overdressed.
Jack Frost arriving, on cold days,
Out with the can of de-icer spray.

Dark are the mornings, carry your torch light,
Suddenly an animal scurries, giving you a fright.
Home-made stews and soup, to warm you inside and out,
Don't forget the dumplings and suet pudding helps.
A nice log fire, roaring up the chimney breast,
What more could you ask for, you're like an animal in your nest.

Marilyn Pullan

HAPPY OCTOBER TO YA!

O ut of the
C louds
T umble d-r-
O -p-s of
B eautiful water
E ver glistening in the
R eluctant sun

Keith Beasley

LIZZIE

A tiny, indomitable woman -
unfazed by the onslaught
of towering north sea waves
crashing over the sea wall -
demolishing the out-house yet again.

White hair - soft as spun silk
pulled tightly into a tiny bun
in keeping with her stature.
And yet when loosed
falling like a coolie's pigtail

Skin like burnished leather
creased and wrinkled
by years of salt-laden air -
and smiles and laughter
and maybe a few tears

Strident bells and raised voices
are the sounds I remember.
the squeal of the aid
clamped to a thin, worn cardigan -
compensating for hearing long gone.

The bell summons her to her duty -
to her front room shop.
The raised voices of customers -
who know the inadequacy
of the squealing aid.

The profits of this shop
are measured in conversation, laughter and tears.
They are eaten up in *Wagon Wheels*
given to visiting grandchildren -
'For the journey home.'

Ruth Walker

AUTUMN

Autumn when Mother Nature prepares for winter days,
When the mornings and evenings have a slight haze.
The temperature is dropping down, down, down,
And all the leaves are turning russet and brown.
Falling from the branches to the ground,
Underfoot they make a crunching sound.
Children collect conkers from the trees,
Broken down by the autumnal breeze.
The animals get ready to hibernate,
Each one caring for his or her mate.
Mornings and afternoons begin to get dark,
No more long walks in the nearby park.
Gone are the shorts and long summer days,
When the sun beat down and seemed to blaze.
People now dress in warm clothes of wool,
As bleak autumn is making the climate cool.
The children reluctantly return to school,
No more playing or paddling in the pool!
Dark, cold evenings of homework lie ahead,
Darker mornings, it's so hard to get out of bed!
Now the heating is being switched on again,
It's getting quite chilly with the wind and rain.
However, it's not all doom and gloom,
There are still some flowers out in bloom,
Reminding us that spring will come back again,
And all the trees will blossom, thanks to the rain.
Yes, the seasons change: autumn, winter and spring,
Then summer, with all its warm, long, sunny days bring.
We welcome each season, they are changeable and new,
Blustery winds, rain, icy snow and warm sunshine too!

Grace Harding

AUTUMN JOY!

Golden autumn days with joy appearing,
Excited frisky winds that come a-blowing,
Trees and their branches swaying and waving,
Bewildered leaves say, 'Goodbye, we are going,'
Falling, falling, in a colourful whirl
Of russet, green-tinged flame and brilliant gold.
Nature's multicoloured, patterned carpet laid,
Bringing a rustling joy for walkers young and old.

Rosy-red apples and green and yellow pears,
Smile and nod vigorously on orchard trees,
Then the frisky winds they come a-blowing,
One by one they tumble and fall on soft leaves.
Rows and rows of colourful vegetables in their prime,
Of orange, white, gold and healthy green,
With joy displayed in churches' harvest festivals,
Autumn season's crowning triumph is seen.

Mother Nature provides also for her tiny creatures,
Acorns, nuts and juicy, rich red berries too.
They busily gather, safely hide their harvest for winter,
This autumn joy feast will see them safely through.
Sunshine now mellows as slowly days grow shorter,
Clocks move back, 31st October, one hour we will gain,
Out come colourful woollies, scarves and brollies,
When frisky winds come a-blowing, and the rain!

If you were born in the autumn like me,
This *is* a special time of joy, you will agree!

Stella Bush-Payne

TAINTED AUTUMN

Someone must know why autumn has such great appeal,
Harvest moons and silver mists, so many hearts to steal,
A welcome winding down from summer's hectic pace
Of longer days spent in the rip-tide of the human race.

If in our autumn you and I could like a leaf be bold,
Life's work done, one last defiant, pointless act behold
Of riotous brazen colour before un-pensioned obsolescence
From senescent host, with no apology for forced redundance.

Instead, like all those less than hardy annuals of death row
Exhausted by the competition, floral drain and seeds to sow
Have aged so quickly and are easy prey
To harsher climate, pestilence and shorter day.

Is autumn nothing more than a reluctant slave
To summertime excesses and disposed-of treats,
That the laden table can be cleared is a major feat
To make way for such dormancy as one might crave?

Down-trodden autumn might forego the role of minion
With destructive deluge, gales, impromptu frosts,
But cap in hand it lopes to solstice and oblivion
All but those so well prepared will bear the cost.

Of the sisters, autumn's not the memorable one,
Often eclipsed by a harsh winter's doleful tedium
A growers' spring or true summer of unending sun,
But to the wise, autumn is not all death's atrium.

Michael Hayes

ABOUT MY FAVOURITE PLACE

Green grass sways in the gentle breeze.
Trees stand tall making sure everything is in place.
Roads run away as if scared by the tranquility.
A wooden bridge arches over a rushing river,
Letting people trample on it as they please.
Horses swat at passing flies, as they doze in the midday sun.

Leaves fall from the tall oak trees, making a golden path.
The sun arrives late, keeping the golden land dark.
Animals start to go to sleep till the end of the winter.

Winter is here now, grey, cold winter.
Paths are sludgy and the river cold.
But however cold, this place stays beautiful.

Benjamin White (11)

LEAVES OF AUTUMN

Summer makes way on the appearance of autumn
As we look out on a picture of change and sight
Gone is the glorious warmth of the golden rays
Bringing the shorter hours of God's precious light
The gardens will soon seem rather faded and bare
As the constant fall of the crisp russet leaves drop
The glories of autumn colour, fast losing their glare
Then it is time for hibernation till cold days stop
And for nature's own creatures to snuggle up deep
It was by God's creation and the decree of His hand
Four seasons were given to treasure, autumn to reap
In the vision of the wide sky and the rich, fertile land.

Octavia Hornby

PRELUDE TO WINTER

Oh summer theatre take your rest and submit to
The next course on Mother Nature's platter.
To walk beneath an autumn sky, escorted by a cornflake shadow.
Presently aware, a velvet richness soon to fall
Victim of the skeletal season.
Grey and white clouds become locked in battle
To take command of the vast area surrounding.
The semi-naked tree stands tall as her fruits are gently grounded.
Along with sleepy hedgerow undergoing
The beginnings of its elemental makeover.
Temporary shadows of former glory
Awaiting evening's premature curtain
Enveloping all of nature's treasures in a soft blanket of grey.
Gentle coolness bathes my inner warmth
And shares with me the beauty and glory of this day.

Virginia Aggett

GOLDEN EVENINGS

I love the crunch of leaves underfoot,
Bushy-tailed squirrels stocking their larders for winter.
Iridescent jays hiding acorns among the leaf litter,
Golden evenings spent in the woods,
Watching the leaves change colour in the dusk.

Nature's paint palette changing from shades
Of green to bronze and gold,
Blood-red and sunflower yellow.

I love the autumn, it is a period of reflection and decay,
Yet decay brings forth new life in the spring.

I love the smells of autumn; the earth, the pines, life itself.
I love spending golden evenings with you, or alone with creation.

Derek Blackburn

OUR NATURE WALK

Spectacular sunrise,
swells, spills,
splashes sporadically.
A cascade of colours
across Earth's crust.

Copper leaves kissing little feet,
dancing joyously.
Twisting, turning.
Laughter riding on October breeze,
caressing tender cheeks.

I falter momentarily,
soul bowed reverently,
in witness to the splendour
of nature's final symphony.

Home.
Cozily cocooned from
falls' fiery bluster.
A field mouse cowers
taking cautionary cover
in our vacuum cleaner.
Not discovered until after . . .
Crunch.

Tracey Rosehorse

WHAT DO I SEE?

When I am at the beach
What do I see and feel?

I have the feeling of freedom
I look out to sea and see space
I feel as if this is how it always was

I want to shout, wave my arms about
I love the sea, waves washing the shore
The open sky, fluffy clouds skipping the heavens

That feeling of peace with wide open spaces
Nothing hemming you in
Just blue sky, fresh air and the wind in your hair

I think the peace is the best
The wind blowing the clouds
Across halcyon autumnal skies

The best of the best
Sea caressing the shore
Gentle breeze, lapping waves
Disappearing into the sand.

Carole A Cleverdon

THE PROMISE OF AUTUMN

Raise your eyes to the sky
On this autumn day,
So you may see the gold.
For the leaves' vivid light
Will shine in your heart
And comfort your gloom away.

As the wind brings the gold
Beneath your feet,
A magical carpet so rare,
It will soften your tread,
And solace your heart,
In a way beyond compare.

Throughout the land
Is this glory spread,
Proclaiming fulfillment of trust,
That will carry us through,
Like a love that is true,
Whatever the winter's thrust.

Mary Hughes

MY AUTUMN

Walking along,
Leaves underfoot and falling from the trees,
Reds, yellows, browns and greens,
This is my autumn.

Cloud and sunshine,
Wind and rain,
Muddy paths and marshy grass,
This is my autumn.

Hat and scarf,
Wearing wellies, I'm walking along.
Acorns and chestnuts on the woodland floor,
This is my autumn.

Wet and cold,
Dog muddy from our woodland walk,
Now we're warm and dry,
This is my autumn.

Nichola Jagus

AUTUMN

Gone are the long, lazy days in the sun,
barbecues and family fun,
back are the short days, with lights on at five,
and the long wait until it gets light,
a welcome end to the drawn-out night.

We complain about the weather,
it's awful again, yet more rain, but desperately hope it will get better.
However, the trees in autumn are a delight,
so many different shades of colour, a welcome sight.

A brisk walk on a crisp day can warm us up,
coffee in a café and a pleasant chat,
smiling at summer memories and planning future holidays
keeps us looking forward to those long, lazy summer days,
longing for them to be upon us again.

Julie Marie Laura Shearing

TO TURN A CORNER

It's as if we've turned a corner
And the once hot summer days have gone.
A new, crisp and colder season has swiftly come along.
Dark now are the mornings as the family travel to work each day,
On go warm, woollen clothes as we pack our summer ones away.
Cool are the days, with a bright, watery sun,
Drawing in of the evenings, when the day is done.
We can close our curtains and shut out the cold night,
The room is warm and cosy, with a fire burning bright.
Curl up snugly in a big armchair,
With blankets covering little toes bare.
Hot mugs of tea, plates of hot, buttered toast,
This is the part of autumn I love the most.

Mary Plumb

AUTUMN

A softness in the air, the evening's misty haze,
The morning's chill, the touch and feel of autumn days.
Great trees, defying winter, give their final show -
Wearing their brightest reds and golds - branches aglow,
Displaying brilliantly - their leaves, abundant now
So soon to fall, will carpet prettily below.
Why do I love this time? What draws me yet again?
A hushed expectancy, a feeling unexplained?
Once in my carefree youth, my spring and summer years,
The thought of wintry days filled me with untold fears.
Bleak wintertime to stretch so coldly on and on -
But in my autumn life those feelings now have gone.
Now I long to feel the comfort and security
Drawing it near, feeling its cosy, warm maturity,
My heart, at peace and warm with autumn's coloured glow
Rests peacefully, serene, for I love autumn so.

Barbara Lovell

FALL

As summer fades away.
Fall is on its way.
Feel the September chill as the leftover summer's sun shows his face
The trees are brown and russet red.
Horse chestnuts on the ground.
The air is cool and clear.
The earth is cold.
Leaves are scattered on the floor.
The whole world's colour has changed.
Mother Earth is clothed in a darker range.
The animals are getting ready for hibernation.
People no more laze outside, bathing in the sun.
But behind curtains and closed doors by the fire.

Rachel Van Den Bergen

LITTER BUGS

I'm just a sweetie paper
lying on open ground,
with many friends and relatives
scattered all around.

It isn't nice being litter,
outside on your own,
battered by autumn wind and rain,
I'd rather be at home.

The next time that you see me,
don't run away and hide,
please pick me up and let folk see
the highland countryside.

You see I have my uses,
for once I was a tree
that now can be recycled
to make paper plates for tea.

When throwing out your rubbish,
secure me, safe and warm,
not left lying in soaking grass,
or blown about by storm.

No matter what disguise I wear,
plastic, cartons, paper, tins -
please lift me gently off the ground
and place me in the litter bins.

Leigh Crighton

BLINDING AUTUMN SUN

Blinding autumn sun
Washes away the dreary fog and glum
Short sleeves out and ditch the tights
All in favour of this new, dazzling light

Crisp-leaved pathways
Lead the way through longer days
Music on loud and sunglasses out
A glimpse of radiance has come about

Soft zephyrs whirl
Whispering at fields and folks to unfurl
Failing flowers dance once again
Lingering rays grasp the day's remains

Fresh, happy smiles
Brighten up their lives' long miles
Distant echoing laughter slowly fades
A gardener sweeps aside the leaves with a spade

One-off summer's day
Did you hear what it had to say?
Or were you too, stunned
And hypnotized by the

Blinding autumn sun?

Anya Lees

AUTUMN GOLD

How happy I was after the grey winter days
To see the budding leaves of spring,
And how grateful in the summer's heat
For the cool, leafy shade of a tree.

But now it is autumn and the leaves are dying,
Falling, falling, flying, flying -
Dying in a blaze of glory,
Russet, crimson, mellow gold,
As though within themselves they hold
The golden warmth of summer's sun.

Soon, starkly etched 'gainst chilly skies
Will stand the trees, leafless and gaunt.
The leaves wither and die, but in the spring
How happy I'll be once again to see
The tender green of a budding tree.

Doris Dowling

THE FIRST LEAF OF AUTUMN

The first leaf of autumn
Free-falling to the ground,
Gliding and swirling,
Hovering around.

Afloat on a current of air
Flying gently by,
Twisting and turning,
Dancing through sky.

Flight comes to end,
Gently touching the ground,
Suddenly a gust of wind,
Once more upward bound.

Ashley O'Keefe

DEATH IN AUTUMN

A faint humming sound in the distance.
The tree's autumn leaves float down,
Filtering over dark branches
And interlacing sunlight,
Drift softly onto the
Cold, crispy ground.
Small beetles scurry and toil
In the dense undergrowth,
Renewing life in the trees
Ancient, gnarled and twisted roots.
And the humming draws nearer.
A robin's sweet, piercing song
Echoes through the tree
And is suddenly still.
Incisive and fatal,
Death arrives.
The chainsaw.

Angy Lindsay

AUTUMN

The tree trembles
farewell to summer
as cool autumn showers
mist the dying season.

Her fraying cloak
bathed in gold sunlight
bares her identity,
and the chilled wind whispers,

and the tree sleeps,
and the last leaf falls.

Josephine Duthie

THE DANCE OF AUTUMN

Autumn dances in,
Kissing old lace effigies
Of leaf formation,
In her constant colour mode.

Yellow, the summer solstice spared,
Red, green and brown,
Now highlighting her death,
Now she's gone,
And dew-filled daisy chains.

Autumn's cup full to the brim,
We dance holding hands
In a fairy ring,
Dreaming on.

Autumn is the face of an old man,
Weary, but vibrant,
With glowing vigour.
Rouge, rough-apple cheeks perchance,
Collating crisp corrosion with stance,
Weaving ashes in his glance.

Whirling, falling, forever,
Coloured leaves,
For this is autumn's dance.

Mary Mullett

THE OUTCAST

The outcast stands old and worn
Amidst the autumn golds and reds
The yellow also shows itself splendidly
On the ground where he treads

A man who lives yet not by choice
In a canvas house with a carpet of grass
May seem to live a wondrous life,
One better than in the past

A common man of dignity and worth
Paid for his crime through protest yet!
A period of time served in gaol may
Not be the worst in life he may get!

And now that time of so many years has passed
The worn old man became an outcast!
No friends, no place to which he belongs
No towns, no cities with their rights and wrongs

Autumn is here as he well knows
Among the damp and wet he shows
So much courage, with so much on his mind
He knows now that it is best forgotten and left behind.

F J Lawton

ALDERBROOK

It's the second week of the flu.
The fever has broken into capsules of sweat
And Mum has opened a window downstairs,
And Dad is watching the Ziegfeld Follies.
And the family's buzzing. It's autumn.
The chestnut tree is branching out into storm,
Nuts, damsons, plums fall to the ground again.
The bonfire's lit within a room that extends
Into the kingdom of Heaven and we are warm.
It's the time of rhubarb tart and apple pies,
Whose aromas fill the soul. Christmas is coming again
And we are waiting for that star to appear
That will end all troubles and begin a new year.
The rhododendrons too will bloom again
And laurel bushes shine in sun. Alderbrook.

David Martin

AUTUMN'S TREASURE

Sunbeams pick highlights in your hair.
You, unaware, nature blessed.
Laughter fills the air around you,
Kicking leaves in autumn's fair.

Twigs and golden leaves fall,
Velcro to your scarf,
Accessorise your fun,
You delight in their dance.

Hazel eyes drink in the day,
Soulful, thoughtful, then laugh.
So easy to please a free heart
Unchained in youth.

Shirley Cawte

AUTUMN RESPITE

The dew-soaked mist clings eerily to the ground
Like a cloak discarded there the night before.
Chilled morning air heralds the break of autumn,
While a weakened sun skyward begins to claw.

As trees, like others now prepare for winter,
Their leaves have turned from green to gold and red.
They flutter in the wind, and when discarded
Form a carpet upon which we all can tread.

Squirrels rush around and store food for survival,
Hedgehogs curl into a ball and go to sleep.
Plants withdraw, and seeds lie dormant as if resting.
In order their life energy to keep.

Autumn is a time of ending and beginning.
The fertile times have ceased, for summer's gone.
Preparations for all things now are commencing,
To ensure that life in future carries on.

J E Davies

THAT AUTUMN FEELING

The wind blows hard against my face,
The summer has disappeared without a trace
No more sun, sea and sand,
The once blue sky now looks so bland,
Gone is the green that filled the trees
It's oranges and reds that now colour the leaves
The darkness remains for those extra hours,
And the once dry air is replaced by showers.
My mood once lifted, now plummets to the floor
As I get that autumn feeling once more.

Charlotte Watkins

A SENSE OF AUTUMN

The savage air bites.
On entering the ebony of morning,
strobe lights penetrate my eyes,
and a cacophony of sound
assaults my ears.
The town ahead,
lit up like a Christmas tree,
looks tawdry.
It promises so much
and delivers so little.
The modest trees,
silent witnesses to the chaos,
are opulently dressed.
As dawn approaches
the weary sky,
spectator of the world,
watches fragments of frost
melt into shining dew.
In a garden
foraging through the fertile
carpet of leaves, the collared dove
seeks nourishment.
My breath, a visible
testament to my existence,
is absorbed.
The lights go off.
I sigh in relief.

Rosalyn Westbrook

BRITISH WINTERTIME

One step forward, two steps back,
'It's set in stone'. That old hack!
Winter's bad enough; the dark, the cold.
Don't make it worse! May I be so bold.
The days get shorter, the nights get dark,
It's time we put a stop to this lark.
Why do we, in winter, put the clocks back?
When doing so only increases the lack
Of daylight for us at the useful end.
By doing so, the yearned for light we send
To the morning, what use can we make
Of it there? I'm never awake
Enough to utilize it aright.
It's far more use to have it at night!
I'm much more awake then. I'm an owl!
Yet I can already hear the howl.
Voices complaining, 'It's all right for you,
But what about us? There are others too!
We are really early birds instead.
By that time of night, we all feel dead.'
Leave as it is, maintain the status quo;
By changing things, the danger is you go
Too far the other way. Where would we be?
No dawn chorus to hear, no dawn to see.
It's only for five months, this 'winter time',
Then back to BST and all is fine.
Do not be SAD, but your joy retain,
Sunny evenings we will soon regain!

Tony Cashmore

THE LEAVES ARE FALLING

The leaves are falling now,
Our summer almost gone,
Those few brief days of sunshine,
They didn't last for long.
But autumn has its special colours,
The reds, oranges and browns,
And soon we'll have a swirling carpet,
Cascading to the ground.

The days are getting shorter now,
The nights are drawing in,
Today we had a first shower of snow,
Though the covering was thin.
But Christmas will soon be upon us,
A magic time of year,
Then we'll face the new year,
And put away our fears.

The first sign of springtime,
The daffodils show their heads,
Brightening up our barren land,
Lifting spirits from their dread.
Springtime's a wondrous time,
The lambs with their ewes,
But for me, all the year is springtime,
As long as I've got you.

Stuart C Rogers

ON HER WAY

I heard a whisper in the trees
As they danced dressed in gold
They all seemed to say, tell not the breeze
But autumn's on her way.
She'll arrive in a fiery blaze
Setting skies alight
With red and gold sunsets to haze
Over the fields and hills.
The river below will deepen his roar
As the leaves tumble down
To caress the forest floor
And blanket it till spring.
Summer birds away will flee
Desperately seeking sunshine and warmth
But they far away will leave me
Although I call after them, 'Don't go!'
Summer prepares to say goodbye
As she packs her carpet-bag
With flowers and bluebird skies;
She promises to return next year
But for now, autumn's not far away;
She'll arrive any day soon
Bringing her own beauty every day
As the year turns once more.

J E Alban

MISTY GLEN

Long gone fields of corn, bluebirds, cricket, warm summer sun.
With a nip in the wind, winter's journey has begun.
Mist-filled glens roll across still waters, reflections of treetops with
golden auras.
Long shadows cast, the squirrel at last, gathering bounty from Heaven.
Nature's banquet lies before him, served upon a rustic bed of orange
and red.
Babbling brook with golden boats, trickles through stones of green.
Birds flying high, as one in the sky, point their way to a far-off land.
The woodland path hidden from view, a rustle and crack underfoot
Echoes through sleepy trees, as watchful eyes look at you.
The stag peers through chilled breath at quarrelsome crows.
A fox tail flashes after scurrying rabbits.
Across the valley, the old log cabin, a welcome light with
Crackling firewood, roast chestnuts and stew.
Silver smoke rising through moonbeams, scribing messages to the stars.
All becomes still as the cloak of darkness falls around,
Until, another day is found.

Chris Whooley

BLOWING IN THE WIND

Sweeping up the falling leaves
They really are a pain.
Collect them in a tidy pile
Then they blow away again.

You find them in the hallway
And lurking under trees.
You think you have them cornered,
Then out comes the breeze.

They blow in next door's garden,
It really is a shame.
I look all coy and smile,
As if I'm not to blame.

I wait until it's raining,
Then a sudden dash I make,
I get them all together,
And then I'll use the rake.

B Cotterill

AUTUMN

The year we hailed as new has now grown old,
late rising sun sets earlier each day,
forgotten winds bring unremembered cold,
doom's prophets tell us snow is on its way.

Not yet snow's cloak to warm Earth's unseen growth,
this is a time of increase - and decline.
Discard and harvest home, we practise both,
saving our crops while nature stays benign.

In cornfields self-supporting stooks no more
form age-old patterns where the corn's been shorn.
Utilitarian combines huff and roar,
blowing out dross and garnering the corn.

Bough-bending fruits, bright against leafy green
bejewel the orchards where yet windfalls lie.
Hazelnuts, nature's unsown gifts, are seen
and blackberries on hedgerows hanging high.

Our thanks, for duty nobly done, old year.
Springtime and summer, their true functions found.
Autumn brings increase ere stern winter's here
to guard creation, ceaseless underground.

Martin Summers

AUTUMN

Autumn is . . .
The most beautiful season
And now . . .
I shall give you the reason
Tiny mice . . .
Cuddle up and go to sleep
In hibernation . . .
Safely for the winter they'll keep.

Falling leaves . . .
In gold, russet and brown
Covering . . .
The earth like a beautiful gown
Crispy leaves . . .
Like a carpet of gold
Kicked up . . .
To the air by children so bold.

The dark night sky . . .
Creeps up without us seeing
Just like . . .
A ghostly, transparent being
There is . . .
A slight chill in the air
It says . . .
'Autumn, we are there.'

Ivana Cullup

AUTUMN WISHES

At last I hear the school bell ring
The autumn term is in full swing
I grab my coat, can't wait to go
To home-cooked stew and coal fire's glow

Along the lane I scuff through leaves
Beneath the vibrant, russet trees
A leaf falls down, I cannot miss
I catch it tight, must make a wish

But no time now, my bus is here
I climb aboard, my leaf clutched near
The next stop comes, on jump the boys
The bus is crammed and filled with noise

I catch his eye across the aisle
A lingering look, a secret smile
But all too soon our journey's done
As I depart, he travels on

No chance to chat or get to know
This boy who flips my stomach so
And now I know my wish must be
Tomorrow he will sit with me

Katherine Hedison

AUTUMN TIME IS HERE!

Warm coats come out of wardrobes
There's a chill in the air at night
And in the early evening
The sky is not so light
The wind howls round the treetops
We quicken up our pace
Leaves dance across the pavement
That our cat just loves to chase
Grey squirrels in the garden
Are busy with a reason
Hiding nuts and acorns
Preparing for the season
Hedgehogs search at night-time
Before it gets too late
Through scattered leaves they rustle
For a place to hibernate
A season colourful and bright
Is starting to appear
Look outside and see -
Autumn time is here!

Helen Farley

THE ARRIVAL OF AUTUMN

As leaves start losing their colour of green, for hues of gold and brown
And trees are starting to shed them all, gently floating down
Where upon the ground like a carpet they lay, for insects and beetles
to hide
Away from hedgehogs searching for food, with young ones at their side
They'll soon be seeking a safe, dry place, to sleep the winter through
And with God's good grace, in spring they'll awake, to start their
lives anew
Migrating birds are gathering on the overhead telephone wire
Their relentless chirping and chattering never seems to tire
They'll soon be off on their journey to find somewhere warmer to nest
While our other native birds stay here and cope with the winter test
The flowers in bloom are beginning to fade, with cold winds making
their mark
The bright sun's rays are now only lukewarm, and daylight soon
becomes dark
We'll soon be donning our woollies, and pull our chairs nearer the fire
With plenty of logs on the hearth, for the heat to rise even higher
Outside it gets ever colder, and gales are starting to blow
But inside it's all toasty and warm, our bodies all aglow
So while we prepare for the winter and look forward to next spring
We'll be thinking of new fauna and flora that this new season
will bring.

Lynda Heaton

THE LEAF

The nights are drawing earlier
The weather has a mild chill
Chestnuts fall to the ground
And the birds begin to flee.

The colours are changing now
Greens turn to reds and browns
The children are more wrapped up
And spend less time with me.

The winter months draw closer
But this time is mine
I am older now and wiser
My skin more crisp and brown.

I am hanging closely to the branch
As my time has come to fall
Slowly, I lose my grip and descend
For this is my time to carpet the ground.

I am fulfilling my part this autumn
As I gently lay to rest, I am peaceful now
Waiting to be underfoot, for I am satisfied
Changing the season from summer to fall.

Laurie York

AUTUMN

With an early chill and a morning mist,
It's a sign that summer has gone,
The trees have put on their autumn clothes,
It's like a picture postcard of rust, orange and gold,
The days grow short, while a watery sun
Tries to climb in the autumn sky,
Never reaching very far before the moon takes over.
An early frost catches the flowers unaware,
As they shrink back into the earth to keep warm,
Children put on their winter coats as the sun forgets to shine.
No need to water the garden, as the
Morning dew hangs around all day,
No more sleeping on top of the covers as
You search for that extra blanket.
Squirrels scurry around collecting their winter fuel,
While birds fly to warmer climates.
A conscientious shopkeeper has
Filled his window with tinsel.

Pauline Dowse

AUTUMN WHISPERS

Another leaf falls to the ground
As autumn whispers in the trees,
Fiery hues are fading, amongst
Earth's eternal seasonal sound.

New and old colours all entwine
As silently the mists now gather,
Thorny hedgerows in nightly garb
Against watery skies, combine.

Shifting shadows, lighter, deeper,
In silver rain, cobwebs shimmer,
As graying clouds gather above
Where mountains rise up steeper.

So softly now, autumn will unfold
Sighing gently for summer's loss,
Its colours becoming less bright
Yet, its loss, sumptuous to behold.

Sue Meredith

Autumn In The Country

As the trees are shedding their autumn crown
Thick they lie upon the ground
A sign that winter is drawing near
Christmas first and then New Year

Swallows are all outward bound
Sun and warmth to be found
The harvest of grain all stored in the barn
Away from the mice that do the harm

The potato crop lifted and boxed away
To be graded on a later day
Cattle from the fields are led
Inside to a cosy bed

The flowers in the garden all cut back
To become compost in a refuse sack
The fruits made into chutney and jam
Harvested vegetables ready for the pan

The squirrels store their nuts away
To feed them on a winter's day
Sly old fox coming out of his den
Looking for a big fat hen

The cats and dogs their coats grow thick
Ready for the winter's grip
Getting ready for Jack Frost and snow
When outside, your skin you feel aglow

The sun is slowly going out of sight
Preparing us for a longer night
Sitting round a roaring fire
What more could your heart desire?

Gwen Dunbar

LATE SUMMER THOUGHTS IN EARLY AUTUMN

Late August autumn yellows
Greet hedgerow, trees and fields
As fruit turns ripe and mellows
And swells the harvest yields;
The summer's gone and swifts fly on;
To warmer lands they part,
Escaping chill,
Though summer still
Is shining in my heart.

Late buddleia and butterflies
Enhance the hips and haws and sloe,
As buzzards slide and glide through skies
Serene in setting sunlight's glow;
Gulls screech and cry on thermals high
Above the cawing rooks and crows,
Tall hollyhocks
And parting flocks
Of swallows in their serried rows.

The last of summer's essence spreads
And lingers soft and warm, unseen
To tinge the russets, browns and reds
Of leaves and berries, all once green
Now withering or ripening
In readiness for frost and rime
Which graces ways
Of time and days
That form the joys of wintertime.

Nicholas Winn

AUTUMN LEAVES

Falling leaves of gold, red,
Green and brown
Lying all over the floor
That the wind has blown down
Leaves of all sizes
Falling like rain from the sky
From trees so tall with
Branches way up high.

Foliage slowly disappearing
As the strong winds blow
Leaves being blown off as
The branches bend and bow.
A sad time of the year as the
Trees are stripped bare
Their leaves of many colours
Scattered everywhere.

Raymond Thomas Edwards

SEASONS TO REJOICE

Autumn winds and rain are upon us now.
Leaves once green and supple turning red, yellow then finally brown,
Crisp crackling sounds are to be heard as heavy feet trample
them down.
Trees standing bare with branches all swishing and swaying.
Strong winds a sign that winter is on its way with snow lying.
The cold chill of winter brings fires burning bright
Children wrapped up warm having a snowball fight.
In these two seasons of dazzling colour and delight.
I find my reason for joy and happiness in the warmth of your light.

Deborah Remnant

AUTUMN

The autumn sun hangs low in the sky,
A flock of geese gaggle as they go by.
Meadow mist hangs low to the ground,
Making a mystic cloak all around.

The sun dips lower into the west,
An autumn sunset with a huge amber crest.
In the twilight between day and night,
More geese in formation on a southern flight.

A hush forms over meadow and hill,
An autumn evening tranquil and still.
Summer's gone, now a chill in the air,
Leaves turn to gold, fall without a care.

As night falls, stars twinkle so bright,
The glow of the moon casting its light.
A vixen's cry makes an eerie sound.
A barn owl swoops silently over the ground.

Autumn is here with us once again,
A shimmer of silver each side of the lane.
Autumn's dawn crisp with an early frost,
A beauty of nature, not to be lost . . .

Alan J Morgan

AUTUMN

In autumn all the leaves turn brown
And crunch beneath my feet.
I like to put my wellies on
And kick them down the street.

Joyce Walker

SPECTACLE

From palest pink through red and gold
More beautiful than can be told
The swirl of leaves along the ground
The colours changing all around.

Wild things filling winter larder
Before frost and snow make it harder
Hedgehogs and dormice prepare for sleep
And moles and badgers burrow deep.

Birds departing, more arriving
All with plans to keep surviving
Dewdrops glistening on the leaves
Lacy cobwebs decorate trees.

The deepened colour of the moon
The evenings drawing in too soon
Tingling fingers and woollen socks
Almost time to alter clocks.

First Hallowe'en, then All Saints' Day
To chase the goblins and ghouls away
Chilly days, brisk walks and hot punch
Warm, snugly clothes, mouth-watering lunch.

Breathtaking dawns, each a surprise
Dramatic sunsets, painters' skies
Rich hues blending - so exciting
Autumn's show always inviting.

Betty Nevell

AUTUMN'S CALL

Our roaring fire
Flames so tall
Herald the start
Of autumn's call

A reddened leaf
The fallen fruit
And a robin
With its breast so cute

Hallowe'en
With its hint of fright
The crackle and bang
Of bonfire night

Seeing conkers
On the ends of strings
And the childhood memories
It always brings

The days
That quickly turn to night
The promise of winter
And Jack Frost's bite

The blood-red sky
That chill in the air
I like to know
That autumn is there

Tony Hucks

AUTUMN MORNING

The downward slope of the year.
On carpet of moist gold,
I walk amongst brazen trees
still clinging to party clothes.
The slow, mournful striptease
as leaf by leaf they fall.
The air wet, I can smell rain.
A hollow, featureless sky.
The harsh cry of a crow echoes
around me, bruising the stillness.
Early morning; day uniformed, undecided.
My thoughts a contradiction.
Endings and growth;
uncertainty and peace.

I contemplate the beauty of decay.

Helen Hudspith

AUTUMN LEAVES

As we walk beside the river, our feet encrusted the autumn leaves
They fell from their branches in the cool evening breeze
All brown, yellow ochre, brittle fragments which above us do fall.
From once lush green branches they fall from trees tall
We walk hand in hand, not long had we met
I thought how you excite me as we glide then yet
I wonder if our new love will last as others had not.
It's been just two weeks and I dream of tying the knot
You lead me to a mound of swept leaves that the gardener had piled
We lay close together amongst the leaves, the wind blowing so wild
You gently embrace me and we kiss so passionately
I swoon with excitement and wonder could you be
The one I will remain with and should I let you carry on
The intimacy so pleasant as we lay in autumn leaves.

Maggie Strong

IT'S THAT TIME OF YEAR AGAIN

It's that time of year again when the nights
Draw in and spiders sit in silvered webs
And mornings come all wrapped in misty white
And the first frosts of autumn clip the air.

And once more children make their way to school,
Some to the familiar, some to the new,
Reminding me of a day long gone, cool
With autumn mist when my father took me

To a school all new. Girls, girls everywhere,
Even one who seemed twice my age and was
In charge of the little ones. She smiled such a
Grown-up smile when my father placed me in

Her care. I remember that day, cool with
Autumn mist. It's that time of year again.

Margaret Hibbert

AUTUMN

Slowly, so slowly, the year is turning,
soon for the spring our hearts will be yearning.
Sadly I know that summer has gone,
cooler now the garden, less warmth from the sun.
Flowers of the autumn are all blooming now,
asters, anemones, rudbeckias take their bow.
Today for the first time, a chilly autumn breeze
ruffled the flowers and rustled the leaves,
leaves which are golden, leaves which are red
beneath my feet, above my head.
There's mist in the morning, drifting and pale
draping the garden, clinging as a veil.
Slowly, so slowly, the garden will sleep
and over the land cold winter will creep.

A J Langton

DISTRACTION

Acknowledging a change in the wind
the fallow deer, having lost their spots
as they now wear their thick grey overcoats
leap gracefully like shooting stars
into the dense woodland glade,
seeking protection from the squall.

Relying on each other for safety
the herd detects the rustling leaves
as they sniff the air, endorsing the change
and preparing themselves.
They ruminate and wait nervously
awake to the beating rain through the trees.

Familiar with climatic changes
the deer sigh relief as the wind
rustles through branches and antlers
comforting them in familiar feelings
leaving them alert to other distractions
perceptive to the nature surrounding them.

Jo Galloway

AUTUMN

Misty mornings, golden leaves,
Swallows go from farmhouse eaves,
Spiders' webs at dawn appear,
Summer's going, autumn's here.
Soon we'll feel the frost's first chill,
See its white on field and hill.
Birds come asking to be fed,
Sun much earlier goes to bed.
Harvest moon so big and bright,
Silver penny of the night.
Followed on by Hallowe'en,
Witches' moon shines on the scene.
Leaves dance, tumbling in the wind,
Nuts are there for us to find.
Blackberries, crab apples too
In the lane for me and you.
Now the year is ageing fast,
As the summer days are past.
Gale force winds and pouring rain,
Autumn's with us once again.

Margaret B Baguley

AUTUMN

Autumn leaves are falling,
Falling on the ground.
If one listens closely
They will not hear a sound.

Autumn can be a cold old month,
One we do not like at all.
Folks can slip on wet leaves
And hurt themselves when they fall.

No one cares for autumn,
0It can be very dark and cold,
But you can be snug and warm
In your own little fold.

Soon autumn will be over,
Then winter will be here,
Then it will be Christmas
And then we all will be full of good cheer.

David Sheasby

AUTUMN

As I walk through the coloured leaves
I look up at the school building
and see the shadows of trees
especially the tropically-shaped flowers
with their amazement of smell.
I sit on a bench and look at the sunshine
shining through the branches
with their yellowy-gold leaves.
Apart from the screaming of the children
All I can hear are leaves
dropping on the wooden benches.

Evelyn Mulvin (10)

NATURE'S GIFTS

A blaze of colours arched through the sky
As a rainbow flickers and passes by.
The sun shines through, like a mirror of light,
To capture the beauty of a natural sight.

Down in the fields, hidden from view
Are mice, voles and rabbits too
An owl on the wing swoops down to kill,
He may not see you, if you are still.

A gentle breeze stirs in the trees,
Shaking their branches, rustling the leaves,
Yellow daffodils standing proud,
Cover the earth with a golden shroud.

Nature has given us riches so rare,
Lain at our feet, a country fare.
Colours of yellow, green and gold,
Displaying her beauty, vain and bold.

Catherine Lambert

MOTHER NATURE'S LEAVING

It's hard to breathe now the oxygen's dead,
all warnings unheeded after all that was said.
We've stifled and rifled the green and the brown,
now Mother Nature is leaving our ground.
The fields, the trees and the hedgerows, all gone,
now just remain in poem and song.
We tried and failed to save the sun,
now the darkness is here and the night has begun.

Rick Oak

AUTUMN MUSINGS

Nights are length'ning, days are short'ning,
    winter's looming, dank and drear,
Leaves will soon turn red and golden,
    each one from its tree a tear,
As they fall, nature's confetti
    at the marriage of a year
Soon to wed with unknown future,
    challenge - or something to fear?
Autumn's glories, fragile, fleeting,
    touch with beauty summer's bier,
Yet remind us we are mortal,
    'though we hold life very dear.

In amongst the leaves lie acorns,
    You will find them if you peer
Closely, also seeds and chestnuts
    which, whilst icy winds may sear,
Cradle life that, come the springtime,
    fresh and vibrant will appear . . . !
Meantime, Christmas brings its message,
    cries in tones both loud and clear,
'Life or death and ev'ry season,
    God in Jesus you'll find near,
Revelling in His Creation,
    share His pleasure - see, He's here!'

David J C Wheeler

AUTUMN LEAVES

In the autumn they fall
Like snow in winter
Causing havoc on the train lines
All over the country

They rain down in their thousands
Giving roads and pavements
A different shade of colour

Children seem to adore them
As they rush to find the biggest
The smallest
And the most colourful ones

To their classrooms they would take them
And have many hours of fun
Painting, drawing and rubbing
Creating different colours in their own unique style

The teachers would then have them mounted
And display them on the walls
They sure look a beautiful sight
As you walk up and down the stairs
And through the halls.

Pauline E Reynolds

AUTUMN

How soon it comes this autumn time
Crunching leaves and glistening rime
Spiders' webs with beads of dew
And dazzling colours of every hue

Sometimes an autumn sun will show
To warm us with its crimson glow
As if unwilling to give in
To darker days and winter chill

The woodland atmosphere has changed
From summer scents in forest glades
The musty oak with golden head
Sheds acorns where our footsteps tread

The birds have ceased their summer song
Except the robin's sweet and strong
The wild geese are flying high
Weaving arrows in the sky

Hibernation will soon begin
With tiny creatures digging in
They'll find some place that's safe and warm
Where no one else can do them harm

But humans with their choices few
Must stay and see the winter through
Brave frost and snow and winter rain
Till hopeful spring returns again.

Doreen Gardner

CHRISTMAS

We are thinking of You this winter
Oh little one so fair,
In a stable manger lying
With Mother and Father there.
We are thinking of stars a-shining
In a winter sky so grey
One star of glorious brightness
To lead us on our way.
We are thinking of visitors coming
Bearing gifts, and bringing joy.
Sharing their loving kindness
With every girl and boy.
      We are thinking of lonely people
      The hungry and poor today,
      What can we do to help them?
      Surely there must be a way?
We are thinking of all Your lessons
Of love and hope for all -
You let us share your birthday
Oh little one so small.
We are thinking of kings and shepherds
And the lost and lonely too,
Can we do ought to help them?
Can we give love like You?
We are thinking of You this winter
Oh little one so fair -
In a stable manger lying,
With Mother and Father there.

Kay Liepins

Misty Forest

No breeze blew to scatter the mist
It stood silent in the morning light,
Threatening and cold, impassive too
The familiar landscape, an eerie sight.

The birds did not sing this morning
Small animals stayed safe and sound,
Every plant saturated with moisture
Dripping and dripping to the ground.

I shivered as I walked my usual path
Barely visible through the grey wall,
My dog seemed uneasy this morning
Staying close was not his usual call.

Then a faint outline appeared ahead
Imagination or reality I do not know,
But my heart beat louder and faster
As my once easy stride began to slow.

My dog softly barked a single warning
Then cowered behind me quivering so,
I peered harder through the intensity
Was this black stranger, friend or foe?

Then suddenly the mist lifted slightly
I breathed in relief what stood ahead,
Last night's winds had broken a sapling
Leaving only a stump there instead.

It was no monster or fiendish ghoul
As my imagination had first thought,
Just a quirk of nature and the storm,
And the destruction it had brought.

George S Johnstone

CHRISTMAS

Christmas Was
Counting the days to Christmas Eve
Not being able to sleep!
Tossing and turning in the night
Hoping to see Santa and reindeers in flight.
Waking up at 5am
Opening presents as quick as you can -
Toy cars for you - for me a pram.
The fire's aglow - the radio's blaring!
The arguments start - we should be sharing.
The day's soon gone - it's time for bed
I'll take Dolly and you take Ted.

Christmas Is
Trudging through the ice and snow
Carol singers at the door
Decorating the tree - putting the fairy at the top
Seeing children's excited faces
When Santa appears in the shops.
Being woken up at dawn
Kayleigh and Jordan's excited squeals
At dolls' prams - and cars with shiny wheels!
Eating turkey and all the trimmings
Falling asleep in front of the telly
Having tea with tarts and pies
And trifles with various fillings
A few drinks - the day is done
The year's soon gone
Come next year - the new millennium!

Norma Spillett

SANCTUARY ON THE BURNING GROUND

The waste ground, the burning ground,
Decades of Bonfire Nights.
A pruning pyre for trees young and old,
Yet no one touched the ancient hawthorns,
Their perimeter regalness encompassing the forest
But one stood alone, near the burning ground.
A sentinel, an oddity, but not for me
My hawthorn sanctuary.
Not like today's hawthorns,
Whose wing branches are clipped into uniformity.
Mine was unique in its form and texture,
Reminding me of a tropical bird,
That covers itself under a cape of feathers.
A dome covering,
As great as any architecture found in the great cathedrals.
My sanctuary
Inside - looking out.
In spring, summer and autumn, I was invisible
Sitting in the deep leaf litter.
My father would often gather the leaves for compost,
So in turn I ate the goodness from the tree.
I gained strength from my sanctuary,
It became part of me.
Forty years on I can still smell that smell,
I am once more, that little girl sitting safe in her sanctuary.
In winter, I still thought I was invisible,
Outsiders could see me,
For red pom-pom hat and scarf stand out
Against the stark bird-cage structure
As snow, black on white, white on red,
White on black, white on white.

Looking up through the branches
As snowflakes penetrate the lattice
Transforming my cathedral sanctuary into a snow palace
Covering the ashes of the funeral pyre on the burning ground white.

Hilary Jean Clark

NATURE'S GIFT AT WAKEHURST PLACE

Drifting and mingling, amid the trees,
Wandering nonchalantly, amongst the leaves,
Red's vibrant colours, varying in shades,
Falling so gracefully, to cover the glades.

Yellow was glowing, bright in the sun,
Could this be autumn has begun?
Gold so pure, with royal tones,
Blending with its magical undertones.

Orange appears to dominate focus,
Striking in richness, as does the *crocus*.
Green so alive, the force of all species,
Calm in its quality, natural as peace is.

Amid the rain our footsteps trod,
Along footpaths, of coloured leaves we plod.
A rainbow appears, with its array of tints,
Caressing the gardens, with a dramatic hint.

Seeking shelter, but hesitant to do so,
This moment in time, felt obliged to vent no.
A moment to appreciate nature's call,
The glory of colours answering the *autumnal fall*.

Even the rain didn't spoil our visit, thank you, it was magic.

Lorna Tippett

AUTUMN GALE

The gale rose stealthily - its only warning
A stirring of the air - a sighing in the trees -
A shiver through the grasses;
But soon, with rising anger, it unleashed its power.
Pouncing - buffeting - howling with increasing rage.
Ripping the hedgerows - scything through woodland -
Crying havoc in the country lanes. Battering - ravaging - destroying -
Until - lust yet unsatisfied - it streaked away,
Bearing confusion to more distant scenes, as darkness dwindled
                                                            to the day.

In the stunned aftershock of violence no bird sang.
A squirrel, his friskiness subdued, scrabbled for hidden nuts uneasily,
Then bore his bounty to some sheltered nook, to feast alone;
While other woodland dwellers, a-quiver through the night,
Warily crept forth to scour the violated meadows.

A few tenacious leaves, surviving the gale-swept hours,
Hung limply from denuded boughs; while those defeated
Carpeted with rich colour their final resting place.
Only the sombre ivy, clasping the shaken trees with leech-firm grip,
Withstood the onslaught and remained unscathed.

A night of devastation - yet, come the spring -
Nursed by November mists - restored through winter's rest,
Woodland and meadow will prove unconquered.
Catkins will dance again - naked trees shake out new leaves -
The hedgerows foam with blossom.
From hidden drey and den newborn creatures will emerge
To sniff - and twitch - and scamper with delight

Among a myriad wild flowers growing in lush grass;
While darting birds nest eagerly, and with ecstatic joy,
Sing Alleluias to the Resurrection scene,
Which mortals faintly echo at Eastertide.

V J H

AUTUMN

Autumn is the time of year,
When nights are dark and cold!
The wind that sings a mournful song,
Like a wandering lost soul!

Sleeping trees that bow their heads
Prepared for winter's sleep
Until the buds peep through the snow
A vigil they must keep!

The days are short, but yet it seems
There's beauty still to see.
Leaves of russet, brown and gold,
Drift down on field and lea!

When daybreak dawns and the air is clear
Maybe frost shines on the ground.
Dressing the land in a cloak of white,
Flowers no longer found.

Time again to light the fire,
And sit in reverie.
To ponder on the coming months,
When spring, once more we see.

Greta Gaskin

AUTUMN

The tiger spider builds his web
Across the old back gate.
There's someone calling to get in
They'll really have to wait.
To break this delicate work of art
Would surely be a sin.

The pale wild geese fly overhead,
With shrilling echoing cry,
Etching V formations
Across the cold blue sky,
Heralding autumn as they head
To feed at the marsh nearby.

Wee Robin takes the swallows' place,
Red leaves drift to the grass
The frost touches the faded rose
And tells that summer's past.
With quiet and colourful majesty
The autumn's come at last.

Frankie Shepherd

CLOUDS

As I watch the clouds by day
I see them gently float away
From where they came I do not know
I wonder how far they have to go
And what will they bring, snow or rain
Or unmasked sunshine for a lovely day.
That magical gift of precipitation
Floats by my window for my own gratification.
My personal show many times a day
Floats right in, then blows away.

Darren Babbage

THERE WILL BE FROST AGAIN TONIGHT

Skeleton trees are sketched in charcoal
  on a backcloth of pale-blue sky,
Where clouds of purple and of rosy hue
  hang motionless on high.
The sun, on fire, goes down in a blaze of glory
  behind the western hill,
Whilst on the shady north-east lawn
  the glistening frost of morning lingers still.
A silver moon waits patiently in the wings
  her part to play;
As darkness falls her call will come
  to light us on our way;
Soon to be joined by a myriad of dancing stars,
  sparkling diamond-bright,
While here below, the January air is bitter cold -
  there will be frost again tonight.

Anita Cooling

REBIRTH

Reaching, stretching to the light,
Unfolding; yawning at the dawn,
Beading dew trickling, tickling tiny petals,
Worms wriggling, brushing hairy stems,
Sap rising, embryos fighting for space,
Peeping; unfurling green chlorophyll flags,
Turning; twisting, sucking the sun,
Flowers opening in the blinking of an eye,
Bristling yellow stamens, wafting scents,
Wanton trick mating calls,
Swaying; scattering, sprinkling new generations,
Dormant, just waiting for their time.

Josh Brittain

INSPIRED BY NATURE

Browns, yellows and burnt umber
Colours warm in the autumn sunshine.
The noise of helicopter wings as dragonflies hover over the pond
Their rainbow iridescence muted,
camouflaged against the bark of the trees
beginning to shed their leaves,
battening down the hatches
against the winds and rains of the coming season.
Shorter days and longer nights
Seasonal Affected Disorder brought only through lack of light.
But not yet.
Enjoy the midday warmth, the lengthening shadows.
The lush green of the grass, moistened by the morning dew
still growing, absorbing footsteps.
Car windows saturated, steaming, dripping
Unsure of the season.
Roses in full bloom against leafless stems.
Can you hear stillness?
Silence broken only by the gentle chirping birds on the wing
The sky blackened by migrating swallows,
some lingering behind on garage beams
only too eager to enjoy the fading sunlight.
Absorb the transient warmth.
Feast the eye on the fruit of the holly and laurel
and the hips and haws of the hedgerow.
Nature enveloping the body and soul.
No turning back, no reversal.
Season will follow season
uninterrupted by Man.
Roller-coasting onwards
Unheeded, undeterred and undaunted.

Gael Nash

THROUGH THE YEAR

Have you ever sat by firelight and dreamed of summer skies?
Of soft gold sands . . . spume-crested waves of blue?
Have you hugged that warmth while, on the ground, a
snowy carpet lies;
And yearned for sight of springtime's soft green hue?

Have you ever watched first snowdrops push their heads up
thru' the ground;
And tiny buds burst forth from stark, bare trees?
Have you listened as the mad, March wind creates its mournful sound,
And watched last autumn's leaves borne skyward on its breeze?

Have you ever seen the sparkle in a raindrop on a rose;
And stroked the silky smoothness of its petal?
Have you ever seen a bullfrog, on a water lily, pose;
Or picked a leaf of dock to soothe the stinging of a nettle?

Have you gazed from rocky headland at the thundering, pounding sea;
Or paddled in the soft, warm brine on a quiet shore?
Have you stared in fascination at the antics of a bee;
As rich, sweet scent of honeysuckle brings him back for more?

Have you marvelled as a rainbow formed its arch when rain was gone;
And matched its hue with a myriad of growing summer flowers?
Or sighed as daisies and dandelions raise their heads, as one,
Across the lawn which you must cleave, between the summer showers?

Have you watched the changing leaves thru' gold and yellow to brown;
And waited for the wind and frost to drag them from their mooring?
Have you contemplated Mother Nature's ever-changing gown;
And thought, like me, that without seasons life would be so boring!

Doris Sproston

THIS WORLD OF OURS

Gaze about at this world of ours
The wonderful birds and trees and flowers
Take time out to look around
So many treasures can be found

Take a walk down a country lane
Your life may never be the same
When we live in the town or city
So much is lost to us, more's the pity

A young child's eyes are full of wonder
Their very first sight of a goose and gander
The mother hen with her baby chicks
Getting up to all sorts of tricks

Cows in the field make them laugh with glee
So many animals for them to see
Horses and goats and pigs in the sty
Don't let the opportunity pass you by

So take your children whilst they're small
Let them climb the stile in the wall
The countryside gives so much pleasure
Happy days, memories beyond measure

This world of ours is a beautiful place
The wonder of nature for us to embrace
The changing of seasons for all to see
So soak up its beauty, it's ours and it's free!

Barbara M Beatson

RAIN

Running its race
I watch the rain
Trickling down
My windowpane.

Joining its friends
They form a line
Increasing the chances
Of bettering its time.

Pitter and patter
The hypnotic sound
As it travels the window
On its way to the ground.

Dripping and splashing
Collecting together
How interesting it can be
Watching he weather.

Rushing in streams
They group to a huddle
Wanting to be next
To land in the puddle.

That is where
Their race it does end
Accomplishing dreams
And meeting a friend.

Joanne Hale

GLORY

I stand strong where I lie,
I have given the world my all
And made it a much better place to live.
Winter is around the corner
And soon I won't bloom anymore for months,
I will sleep here where I lie.

I hope they will remember me and the joy I gave
And they won't throw me away.
When winter comes I am but a stick in the ground.
From stunningly beautiful blooms and shiny leaves
I am cut down, I fight back
But winter says no to my efforts to bloom again.

One might say I am dead, stripped me of all that I am,
Reduced me to nothing,
Then when spring comes He will give it all back to me in
one giant swoop.
I am resurrected to new life. I was dead and now I am alive,
I am stronger and more beautiful than ever.
You will want to pick my blooms once more.

Jean Bailey

WEEPY WILLOW

The mournful tree
raped of its beauty
by the winter breeze
Disowned by the proud bird
and now abandoned by the summer sun
However, worry not and weep no more
for I promise very soon
Mother Nature will make you
beautiful once more

Ian Benjamin

COUNTRYSIDE

Bright morning sun,
ripe blackberries,
the falling leaves,
early-morning mist,
cluster of ripe nuts.
An autumn landscape,
a clear blue sky.

Scarlet berries,
carpet of moss,
purple heather on the moors,
russet, gold and brown leaves,
extremely frosty.
All the glories of the countryside.
Away to the north in all its glory.

Anita Shedlow

BIRDS

A beautiful garden
What a wonderful sight
The birds all around me flutter
I see them proudly open their beaks
But to me not a sound they utter
I love to see them flying free
And thank Him above that I can see
These wondrous creatures large and small
I dearly love them, one and all
I cannot hear, but I can see
How glad I am, that I am me.

Agnes Driver

THE GARDEN

In winter, summer, spring or fall,
The garden is a place for all;
Nature, in her own sweet way,
Makes life worth living every day.
The humble pansy, white or blue,
And even some with purple hue,
Can fill your heart with pure delight,
As they then dance in the morning's light.

The rose, a majesty of bloom,
Will cast away the darkest gloom,
In vibrant shades of pink and red -
So rich and regal in their bed.
The busy Lizzie, all should know,
A common flower so many grow
In baskets, window-boxes and tubs,
Or even, to enhance our shrubs.

The fuchsia with its dainty bells,
It seems to me a story tells.
For when the breeze moves them around,
You'd swear, that you could hear the sound.
Some gardens have a waterfall
That cascades down, admired by all.
Others have a grand round pond
Where fish they swim and frogs are spawned.

Come winter, with its ice and snow
A time we plan what next to grow,
To dream of what the year will bring
While waiting patiently for spring.
The garden where you grow your flowers
Gives pleasure great for many hours;
A gift, from Mother Nature sent,
The owner her, to you just lent.

I A Morrison

WINTER'S HERE

When autumn's rich abundant glow
Is dimmed as north winds start to blow
And compost heaps of damp brown leaves
Lie at the feet of bone-bear trees
Winter's here!

When skies are bleak and dark as night
Without the sun to shed some light
And cheery robins in vests of red
Appear in gardens to be fed
Winter's here!

When fingers, toes and noses too
Are nipped with frost and turning blue
Hats and scarves we must adorn
With extra clothes to keep us warm
Winter's here!

When singers bring the Yuletide cheer
With carols that we love to hear
On Christmas Eve - 'Oh silent night'
The eastern star shines ever bright
Winter's here!

When holly is seen with the mistletoe
When Earth is covered in soft white snow
When gritters are caught on the hop
When traffic comes trundling to a stop
When things have grinded to a halt
Who's to blame, who's at fault?
Oh dear - oh dear, it's so austere
Now winter's here!

Carol Kaye

THE OAK

From my window
I see the majestic oak
clothed in a mantle of leaves,
pregnant with acorns.

A great earth mother,
she sheds her offspring
without a second thought
for where they fall.

Demanding nothing from them -
she cares for them no more.

Winter comes -
she shakes her leaves free,
having taken her sustenance from them,
no interest now in their destiny

Facing the bitter icy winds,
strong and upright in the gales.
Allowing nothing to sway her,
she stands - proud and bare.

I watch with admiration,
and wish she was my mother.

Rose Ashwell

A WORLD FULL OF NATURE

This world was created many, many years ago
Long before any one of us could ever know.
It's full of so much beauty, for all to see
From the lovely mountain tops, to the little flying bees.

This world is full of beautiful things that always look just right
All those lovely flowers full of colour, and so bright.
All its splendour and glamour will always make our world so
beautiful and bright.

This world full of nature, for all of us to see
But many take for granted the beauty within any tree.
Just look around you, when you're out and see the lovely world created
That many of us are trying to destroy,
This world was created for us to never destroy but to enjoy.

So just take a moment each day whenever you're out
To enjoy the beauty deep within this world of ours,
Before someone takes it away from us within an hour.

Hatred is a terrible thing for anyone to do
But it happens in this world of ours and what can we do?
If only those who show their hatred, could turn to love
They would see this world of nature, was created by God above.

Anastasia Williams Cowper

COLOURS OF AUTUMN

Blood-red and damson purple
waving upon high,
golden sand and mustard yellow
whisper with a sigh.

Crimson haze and bottle green
clinging where they dare,
rosebud pink and purple heather
destined to stand in despair.

Soft and gentle breezes
loosen up the wings,
cold and rain sweep through,
their voices sharply sing.

Feather-light they fall
towards a sodden earth,
leaving at their allotted time
having spent their worth.

Blood-red and damson purple
no longer on a high,
golden sand and mustard yellow
cast off and set to fly.

Crimson haze and bottle green
no more to cling with flare,
rosebud pink and purple heather
are soon to find repair.

Mary A Knapp

THE COUNTRYSIDE

The countryside is dying fast
All around is fading grass
The trees so tall are all cut down
To rape this land for common ground

Our landscape change to make again
They take away our leafy lanes
There all around they make the change
With concrete for our country lanes

This land we used to walk upon
So soft and green now all is gone
The concrete now beneath your feet
So hard and cold when e'er you meet

This land of ours we must not part
But keep it safe within our hearts
The time will come when we will see
Just open space not a single tree

This land will be so bleak and bare
Not a flower growing there
No colours there to look upon
It's still all grey in the morning sun

So to this land bring warmth and light
The flowers will grow in the early light
The birds will sing across the sky
And all our hearts will open wide.

R Claxton

THE RESERVOIR

The gentle breeze
The reservoir, its waters softly lapping on its shore,
Near silence.
In the fields birds calling, a dog barking from afar,
Near silence.
In the sky high above the hills, a buzzard gracefully soaring,
Near silence.
Here I stand in awe, of the beauty that surrounds me,
The colours, the smells, the sounds,
Near silence.
At night the hoot of an owl, the stealthy passing of a fox,
The crow of a cock at dawning,
Near silence.
It is no wonder that the buzzard soars high above a place
of such tranquillity,
Home again,
Pure silence.

Chris Houckham

AFTERMATH

A bridge, whose falling guillotined
a ship that trusted it to hold,
now bobs as a mess of floated steel
all trashed and whitened by the cold.

The ship, cross-sectioned as a blueprint,
goes down in two. The river sighs
and shuts its two banks tight to lock,
its trophy in a case of ice.

Sasha Z Foreman

RED LINES

Evening
and as I gaze up to
the west
thoughts on overdrive.

The sky
a page from nature's
drawing book
to flick through and admire.

As the thin sunset clouds
stretch line-like
across horizon's surface
my imagination speaks,

'Sketched there
in colour
by steady hand of God.'

Kevin Welch

BESIDE A FROZEN POND

Down beside the frozen pond,
Cold water suffocating all beneath,
Hands bitten by winter's maw
Breath now physical, receding.
Before life's broken bond,
Nothing moves upon the heath;
Branches curl into bitter claws
In the place where death's succeeding.
Beside the pond that was thawed in summer
It was warmer when we walked by.

David Woods

IT'S WINTER

Light the night, bright neon sun, the street where shining rivers run,
from salted snows.
Where dwellings clothed in frosty skin, show evidence of life within,
From window glows.
Gardens framed by wall and fence, look forward to the recompense,
Of distant spring.
And shadows deep as mystery, fill the town and wait to see,
What day may bring - it's winter!

The farmstead's wrapped in silent white, there's been a steel hard frost
last night no signs of thaw.
The dog keeps warm as best he can, and cats all wait for the
porridge pan,
Round kitchen door.
Beasts with breath like swirling clouds, their backs all covered in
rimey shrouds,
Blare out for hay.
In field just over blackthorn hedge, comes sound of lads with
home-made sledge,
Enjoying play - it's winter!

Scores of stores, with goods to sell, variety we've come to know
so well, so much to see.
Pavements glazed by slanting sleet, tease the hurrying, scurrying feet,
Of humanity.
Overcoat and wheezing throat, boot and hat and glove denote,
The icy chill.
And roaming youths in fashion gear, like ships without a way to steer,
Have time to kill - it's winter!

Gusty wind and ragged sky, coal black crows, fighting hard to fly,
homeward bound.
Tossed by storm they lift up higher, burnt papers rising from a fire,
Without a sound.
Air like crystal, frozen field, bare bone ash trees, forced to yield,
Their autumn gold.
In countryside and busy town, the dark time season settles down,
A realm of cold - it's winter!

Robbie Ellis

NATURE'S WAY

Midst the amber autumn shades,
Amongst the oak and hazel glades,
Where dwelt in days departed long,
Children of mirth and family song.

Where verdure thrived in rich array,
Once bathed in beauty, now decay,
Nature has again resumed her throne,
O'er the vast changes of ages flown.

Where fruit trees stood in elegant grace,
Now a barren wasted space,
Each stone where weeds and ivy climbs,
Reveal some oracle of happy times.

Now, many have gone with passing time,
Departed beyond to that glorious clime,
Yet, for those who still remain,
The severed chain may link again.

Isaac Smith

AUTUMN DREAMS

Autumn leaves fall in autumn dreams,
where beauty is as magical as it seems.
Reds, browns, bronze, russets and golds,
falling in each day that unfolds.
Falling in the afternoon,
beneath the stars, and silvery moon.
Falling in autumn's mist
in autumn's harvest.
Falling with the chestnuts, conkers, acorns and apples sweet.
The combine harvester gathers the rye, barley, oats, wheat
and sugar beet
Falling while the field mice are at play,
in each of autumn's glory day.
Falling while the squirrels find nuts to store,
the birds' sweet song you hear no more.
Autumn leaves fall, while spiders crawl.
They weep before winter's sleep.
They're blown high into the grey skies,
before they say their goodbyes.
They fall while children play trick or treat on Hallowe'en
fireworks light up the night-time sky, red, blue, pink, orange,
purple and green.
They rustle in the breeze, in the evening's shadows,
before winter's echoes.

Joanna Maria John

FROZEN LAKE

Deep dark waters edged
with dull unmoving shallows -
bank wears ermine shroud.

Perry McDaid

SEASONS

Now the winter fast approaches,
Withered is my field of dreams,
Sadness in my heart encroaches,
Shattering souls, the vision screams.

Summer's halcyon days have ended,
Autumn steals with latent shade,
Gold and brown to amber blended,
Winter's chill soon to invade.

Life to barren landscape harnessed,
Never more will spring resurge,
Time has gathered in my harvest,
Dreams too late to re-emerge.

Days drift down to final number,
Shiver under laden sky,
Wreathed in snow-clad icy slumber
In my field of dreams I lie.

Dorothy Neil

AUTUMN

The leaves are falling off the trees,
It's time to get on hands and knees
And put them all into a sack,
Where light and air there will be lack.
They will mulch down and in a year
Some lovely compost will appear.

Rachel E Joyce

SILENT NIGHT

A silent night when all is calm,
A stillness lies with frosty sight
While all about lie caught in icy teeth:
No struggle; no conflict; no fight,
But only foolish ecstasy that winter
Holds us in its cold barbaric night.
It spreads its wings and soars above its realm
Warning all of immeasurable might:
Might that watches cities fall;
Might to rip and tear and bite;
Might that stirs in hand with Death;
Might of winter - impossible might.
In a parting of silent wings
Lie the secret fears of night
That slash with claw and tooth and nail
And breathe on pleasant thoughts of light.
Then alights the bird of prey
To end the miserable plight
Of suffering, with a quiet kiss
To drop them from a mortal height
Into his dark abyss of snow.
Watching, freezing stars at twilight
Of a vivid summer's days.
All his countenance is frozen greed and spite
As he departs, destruction in his wake,
Leaving no footprints in the glistening white
That speaks with all it owns of Christmas joy;
There endeth life and light.

Katie Hale

COLD COMFORT

Darkest days of winter
gives food for thought -
a moot point,
for the doom and gloom merchants.

Tiptoeing
across the cool kitchen floor,
to fill the kettle
for a cup of tea -
I hear the wind
sniffing around the door,
like hungry dogs
sniffing around for food.

A picturesque veil of frost
on the roof,
belies the cosiness
beneath the loft -
21 degrees
in the living room.

The radio sings
in relaxing mood.

Some frosty footprints
leading to and fro -
those tell-tale signs,
of where the postman trod.

Olliver Charles

EMERGING FROM THE DARKNESS?

I have stood true here for so many years
And fulfilled my purpose with love and cheer,
Surrounded by others, just like me,
Campaigning for fresh air and the right to be free.
I have watched the seasons come and go,
From the new life of spring to the hibernation of snow,
Weathering all of nature's calling card,
It's been a pleasure, although sometimes hard.
For it was expected, I knew how it would be,
It is the wrath of humans that really scares me,
As I heard a message on the breeze,
That this existence should be seized.
For I may not die from a natural disease,
Instead be slaughtered so Man is appeased.
This realisation shook me to my very leaves,
For not all want to preserve - us mighty trees.

Sara Church

WINTER

Across the North Atlantic wastes
the Arctic wind whistles,
moaning 'neath its load of snow,
as Britainwards it rolls.

Grey-wrapped in sky-covering cloak,
it marches on to meet
mountains, hills and vales;
until exhausted, at last
it stands silent and still.

As dawn breaks over British soil,
the sun smiles to see
such awesome albescence.

Joy Morton

THE PLEASURES AROUND US

Some of the nicest things in life are free
Like the sound of the wind, as it blows through the trees
The daffodils nodding in the day-time sun
Simple things that bring us so much fun
A baby's first cry as it enters the world
All simple things that we cherish on earth
The sound of laughter as we hear children play
The smell of the rose and the sun with its rays
The rainbow in the sky that comes between the showers
Seeds that we sow that turn into flowers
All these pleasures in life that are free
The treasures all around us are here for us to see
The joy of the birds as they fly through the air
Animals that roam without any cares
The fall of the rain that makes the plants grow
Snowflakes that come and lay down as thick snow
Trees sprouting out their new shoots in the spring
Baby birds leave their nests and learn how to sing
The green of the grass, the ripple of the stream
The mountains so high and the air that's so clean
Yes the simplest things in life are free
We take them for granted and don't really see.

Margaret Ward

THE SNOWDROP

Winter's death, spring of life,
children of the churchyard, pure bridal white,
transplanted into gardens, companions of the trees.
Haunting screams of distant fox, frosted breath, unyielding ground,
shivering, green-lined petals, clothe the pale winter sun.

K J Hooper

SO SMALL

I feel so small, when I look out at the ocean,
I have no notion of its vastness; width and breadth.
Wonderment bowls me over,
When I view a supernova,
I'm minute, finite, out of depth.
I'm humbled when I hear a roll of thunder,
And lightning licks its way across the sky;
My perceptions seem to go asunder,
Nature's floor show leaves me high and dry.
I'm a leaf in a mighty forest,
A flea in a feline's fur,
But I put myself in motion,
And swell out of proportion,
When my daughter calls me Daddy, I start to stir.

Warren Fraser

JACK

Jack Frost came by last night to me
with all his magic wizardry.
Cathedrals drawn on windows plain,
candles hung on weather vane.
Perfect images drawn in ice,
Leonardo's prodigy drawn to vice.

Jack Frost came by last night to me
with all his magic wizardry.
Jack Frost, Jack Frost your wonders unfold
I see your genius - I touch it gold
I see your breath - I cannot hold.
Jack Frost came by last night to me
with all his magic wizardry.

A Dyas

WINTER

The once healthy leaves on your tree are now falling
As shorter and chill grows your day
Little bird, the first wintry winds are now calling
To lone little you, 'Come away.'

All the eggs you once had in your nest, are now gone
Or maybe there never were any.
Now you perch on the branch of your tree, all alone
Just quiet and sad like so many.

For the too-short contentment of summer has gone
And the feverish spring is long past
The cold wind is here and it won't be too long
'Til the frost brings you peace, at last.

But what of the days in-between, little bird?
Those precious few days still to go?
Is there no one to share your cold perch, little bird?
To give you some warmth in the snow?

Someone to comfort you when the ice comes
Someone to perch by your side
Someone you know will be sad when you're gone
And will finally lie by your side.

Brian Henry

HAIKU

Bare birch streamers weep
   for the dead year. Cloud-backed doves,
     dirge-dark, sit shivah.

Margaret Henning

URBAN STORM

A gathering storm pools over the city
Melding the drowsy blues and greys
The tranquil scene soon joins me in misery
Aloof on a balcony while cold city sleeps

The clouds form an endless shield of grey
Rolling in sync like soldiers to battle
Urges of thunder disturb my trace
Transmitting their deep, subliminal tongues

A chorus of rain then rattles to life
Descending a maze of awnings and gutters
Ribbons of waterfall spill from the roof,
Distorting an image of huddling birds

A church's steeple exposed by lightning,
Its drooping bell immune to the wind
Black garden gates, aglow with wetness
Aging paint flaking off in the clamour

Streetlights stretched across glistening pavement
'Midst an infracted mirror of puddles
Raindrops scratch at draped window clones
Massaging the temples of a world-worn mass

Back in my room the symphony muffled
Thunder runs through a vaulted ceiling
Orange light from a lamp gives warmth
As shadows of water stream down the walls

These rainstorms act as mobile seasons
Passing dimensions that alter the mood
Held in trophy these opulent glimpses
For painter and poet, a window of rebirth.

Brandon Gene Petit

WINTER'S PASSING

Across the way from my abode
a simple garden colder grows
where green abounds in autumn's chill
with brown and golden glows.

Where tit and robin lively flit
in search of human gift
their antics free and pleasing
our flagging spirits lift.

Where leaves in multi-coloured hue
weave and wave in freshening breeze
as if to whisper, balmy days are gone
and winter is overdue.

Where poplars standing tall and proud
liken to sentinels and loudly shout,
'We'll be here come the spring
however deep the winter's shroud!'

Where in a corner, shelter warm,
from coming snows and angry storm
defending all on foot or wing
the holly, ever green and strong.

Beneath soil and stone in frosty grip
in slumber soon to winter pass
it is nature's way to save a soul
the one who sleeps till spring's return.

This time of darkness cherished not
for hallowed reasons comes to test
so others sleep and take their rest
until once more we're blessed with spring.

Eric Langford

THE FROZEN LILY POND

The sky's twin is frozen: it has
    water-soldier clamped,
bubbles clotted as horn, the stars
of duckweed as inert as dust
    and no sense of depth.
The grass I'm standing on is laced
with hoar - January seems set
    on the key of grey.
A few steps - near where the muds meet
the busy path, though quiet still.
    Ignore the beer can
shining and this is an idyll
of winter countryside, in town.

A squabble of crows on their lanes
    of brittle air tells
like carillon; above the sun's
a waste of blue with cirrus tress
    from any season.
The pond, with bleakly marbled glass,
still is a place to be alone,
    unfrozen, and healed -
beyond the stupor of routine
with its bridles of restlessness,
    mock suns of profit -
here the prospect awaits, no less,
of water's returning minuet.

Chris White

SNOWMEN

Dreams in meltdown mode
Hopes of crystalline immortality
Oozing transparent blood
Brevity has existence

Flickering perceived outlook
Shadows extend blindness
Trench-covered wasteland
Engulfed by winter

Minds frozen in anger
Over summers ill spent
Hot metal shatters
Fragile silhouettes

Cold enveloping reason
A scape so drowned
White turns red
Tears stillborn

Stark black faces contrast
Numb feet shuffle mutely
Windows sunk so deep
As to bury souls

Slowly the snowmen melt
Better than painful death
More snow forecast
Generals are like children

John Marshall

WINTERTIME CONTEMPLATION

December's grey and misty horizons disturb the mind,
Wondering what climatic extremes may lie before us
Until their suffering's redeemed in healing realms of spring
But other dreads of time - in heartfelt tears within - I pray for
Those trends of self-indulgent lifestyles that cloud Man's future
Has it become old-fashioned now to pursue healthy moral paths?

As unborn children queue for times of viable appearance and potential
How sufficient an inheritance of enhancing values will they receive
Or could uncreative elements stultify their start - like unhappy orphans?

Now bring new visions for an uplifting springtime of life reborn
Let's find our stronger motivating courage and determination
To firmly leave behind the darkness of destructive influences
As we welcome joyful Christmas carols and sincere new year resolve
Those winter winds of cold indifference cannot blow forever

Before us -
Nature's spring of fresh flowering crocuses and daffodils
So awe-inspiring - and too beautiful by far -
For Man - to forget!

Don Harris

WINTER CAME

Autumn left with the falling of the leaves.
Winter came with a chilled, frigid breeze.
Colours darken to grey,
Heralding change at the remains of the day.

Tendrils of green creep in through cracks,
With stealth that the summer always lacks.
Winter brings the snow that is desired,
And crystal beauty rarely admired.

Aisha Opoku (17)

120

BYGONES

The tennis net is down
And all last summer's sunny players gone,
A once idyllic landscape filled with rain.
The ancient court seemed cracked for different purpose in the sun.

A tree is black and white and bald
And spidery, which once effused;
Framed portraits, dusty, idle, dumb and old,
Stare at where originals had gathered and enthused.

I see this in my gazing from a room.
Behind these curtains memory is confined
While outside the rain falls faster,
Splintering like silver static on the ground.

Richard Kitchen

WINTER LANDS

Bitter, bleak winter arrives,
Sleighing begins and the temperature dives,
For now is the season to be jolly,
Celebrations begin with mistletoe and holly.

Greasy are the roads for sledging and skating,
All month children pray, watching and waiting
For the red man to land with parcels and show,
Making most feel merry, leaving others feeling woe.

For winter is not always the season of just,
For some it is an occasion of loneliness and dust
To settle on the past, memories and lives,
People who've lost children, husbands or wives.

Katie Cheetham

H₂O HAIKU

These fine, white snowflakes
Fall onto mountain scree slopes:
Winter frozen springs.

This bright stream flows down
Through wide, green flood plains, seeking
The cold, dark ocean.

The sun draws moisture
From seas and farms and forests:
In cold skies, clouds form

And fine, white snowflakes
Fall onto mountain scree slopes:
Winter frozen springs.

Alice Boden

WINTER'S DAY

Winter's day,
Sun shining,
View across the hills,
Makes me think of you
Far away.

A pheasant ran across
My path
I let it go free
And that is how I
Want to be.

Oh yes; it's a
Winter's day
And you; You
Are so far away!

Ruth Holder

WINTER

The winter season has arrived again,
the bitterly cold nights never end.
it's my favourite time of year because
it seems quieter and Christmas is near.
Sitting at home on a cold winter's night,
with the central heating on and the little light.
Enjoying a glass of lager, port or sherry,
watching a really good film on the telly.
Eager to go out more to a pub, restaurant or café,
because there is not a lot of people around,
I know it sounds a bit funny.
Me and my mum went down town to
see the Christmas lights be switched on,
we had a few hours of fun and then we came home.

Lisa Anne Oram

WINTER

Winter has become
and my heart getting warmth
I see pure whiteness
which covers my town
and makes it a place from a legend.
There are snowmen who are new citizens
with big smiles.
Snowflakes are miracle materials
that children use to build their own castles.
There are lots of treasures of ice
that make rich my town.

Meldin Trtovac

OH WINTER, YOU LIE IN WAIT

Oh winter, you lie in wait for future days
As autumn swiftly rides away with crisp frosty
Morns, warmed by the sun by ten am leaving
Behind amber and russet leaves with tints of
Green and black dots of blight stealing life
Decaying within another season's time.

Oh winter, you lie in wait and nip our days
With frosty coats of whiteness until you can
No longer let the rain fall without touching it
With snow, the purest of flakes that lay
Our roads to ice and ground to stone
With freezing winds that numb and moan.

Oh winter, you lie in wait to make me slip
My car to skid on the roads that you now own
You breathe your misty coldness to the fields
In cloaks of ice-white curtains till the
Movement of the day reveals in its touch
Of warmth your furrowed snow remains.

Oh winter, you lie in wait to freeze the toes in
Tights and fur-lined boots, try as you may, my feet
Will tread that treacherous sparkling diamond
Path, I crunch you beneath my feet and laugh
Then feel your tears melt off my roof and see them
Dripping from above.
Oh winter, you lie in wait outside my lonely door
Your season shrouded my broken heart four years
Ago but I still love each fresh new scene
You bring to show life can go on. You free my soul
And I know that you have built me a wondrous
Winter palace, my toast drunk, cheers to you
Out of my ice crystal chalice . . .

Oh winter, you lie in wait . . . What will you bring?

Susan Carole Gash-Roberts

WEATHER VANE

Hapless weather,
A forlorn day,
As icicles glimmer,
Feather-light in lost cloud
Hold out for thunder,
In between a cloudy break.

The weather vane,
Trembling intermittently,
Almost folding,
Never leaving me,
Should I depart
I never fail to remember you.

I always like the bracing chill,
The wintry daze on cold cobble slabs,
Aided and abetted by the torque;
A sunny face on your wind,
Dew always gives me hope,
The climate remains perpetual.

I have always been a hoarder,
As long as I remember,
These days I prefer nostalgia,
Money left to build slowly,
Providing for some future
In gardens past like yours.

I have little to liken
Towards the weather vane that I might have bought.
It was lying on a pile
Of household debris in a courtyard;
Leavened by bric-a-brac,
It spoke to me and almost called.

Anthony Cocking

AS WINTER COMES

As skeletons, the once green trees,
Like sleeping giants loom -
Against the stormy, greying sky,
So hushed, yet filled with gloom . . .

Vistas of the twilight fields,
Awash in glistening frost -
North wind blows, his power he wields,
Fall's remnants wildly tossed . . .

Deep within the forest's glades,
Cold silence fills the air -
As creatures lie in beds they've made,
Asleep with not a care . . .

Grasses bow to chilling gales,
Their frozen blankets borrowed -
Withered summer's flowers pale,
Heads bent as if in sorrow . . .

Hardened earth beneath one's feet,
Whilst 'cross the fields you go -
Life seems lifeless, bittersweet,
As it waits the coming snow.

Sandy Tomeo

EARLY WINTER IN SUBURBIA

Early winter in suburbia,
the commuters are still entombed at work
and an elderly man leisurely walks his dog
as two old shopping-laden women
chat almost gleefully about death and dying.
The clouds will turn magically orange when the sun sets
and the leaves strewn on the damp grass
gleam like diamonds when the sun
catches the diminutive raindrops.

White-fingered clouds feather the winter sky,
it's time to reflect on days gone by.

The azure sky entices me outdoors
but a raw razor-wind cuts into me
and a dark cloud briefly catches the sun,
the cloud losing its dullness and now shining
with a most celestial glow.
Shadows slide across the suburban hills
like a tide surging up the sand
but I've escaped from the choking claustrophobia
of toil in the heaving city down below.

Guy Fletcher

A WINTER'S IMPRINT

The air is so rich with this cleaning tool
Which states, 'Out with the old and in with the new'.
Were the air to be coloured it would be frosty blue
Showing the true festive spirit now in full view.
Branches now sag under the heavy white snow,
A robin digs and looks for the red berries below.

Like jewels, icicles hang from the trees,
Crisp ice crackles from under the snow and the leaves.
Early morning smoke from a lone chimney pot blows
Reflecting the warmth as the inner hearth glows.
Tree lights adorn windows as the dawn chorus alights,
Frost paints ornate patterns upon the windows now bright.

Trees are stripped naked without valour or vice,
A few bronze leaves remain, now stiff with the ice.
Meadows turn into golden seas as the countryside slows,
Hares run freely and pheasants fly with the crows.
Foot trodden imprints embellish the snow,
Imprints of all kinds does Mother Nature show.

Darryl Benson

WINTER IS HERE!

From season to season, the year follows on,
Winter is here and autumn has gone.
From mountains to valleys, we travel through life,
For freedom and joy will come after strife.
Autumn is splendid with colours ablaze;
Then comes the winter with frost, snow and haze.
Autumn was colourful, winter is dark.
Autumn was friendly but winter is stark.
The trees may look empty, with branches so bare,
But like Christmas gifts, surprises are there!
Take off the wrappings and what do you find -
Spring has arrived, and winter's behind.
For each season prepares for what is to come,
Like life's ups and downs, or the rain and the sun.
The buds and the blossom were wrapped tightly inside
Until bursting out, no longer to hide.
So do not despair, for hope will return,
With boughs swathed in blossom, from which we may learn
The life cycle continues and it will not stop -
As one pedal goes down, the next comes to the top!

Christine Lemon

THE COLD SPELL

The only people walking the streets are the brave and bold.
It's a winter's day and bitter cold.
The wind direction has turned north east.
It's as though someone's unleashed a beast.
Icy winds that cut through the body, right down to the bone.
Each gust that blows, brings an involuntary groan.
Now is the time to put on that silly hat,
The one you think makes you look a prat.

With the wind comes the snow,
This is the start of a huge go slow.
In the countryside it might look pretty.
Not so, when you have to get to the city.
Children play with energies abound,
While old people are frightened to move around.
Not much fun either if you're driving in your car.
With blizzards and drifting, you'll not get far.

Frost and ice is another part of the cycle,
With frozen ponds and glistening icicles.
Ice turns road surfaces to glass,
Driving safely becomes a farce.
Scraping screens and spraying de-icer,
Summer travel is so much nicer.
Other countries seem able to cope,
While here we seem to give up hope.

With the wrong type of snow or leaf,
It only adds to the aggravation and grief.
Not enough roads are ever gritted,
With minor ones being omitted.
Schools that have to shut because of the cold.
Hospitals that fill up with the old.
Hopefully the summer will be better.
No, this is England, it'll be warmer but wetter.

Robert Humphrey

WINTER NIGHT

Listen to the silence as it sneaks between.
I, the scarecrow stand, like a knight of old protecting the land,
stoically silent in the storm.
Wind rattling through my ribs.
Faithfully. Fearlessly. Battered.
Bedraggled hair hangs limply from my hat.
My button eyes and carrot nose drip softly.
My arms and legs astride. Welcoming
as little, snuffling mice and scared starlings ιιde within me.
The freezing, fresh fields lie bare. Sodden. Soggy.
A chilly bed at my feet.
Slowly, slipping, slithering, slimy
mud engulfs my toes, moulded in potter's wet clay.
I watch the trees.
Lanky, leggy, lofty, like skinless skeletons.
Guardians of the roots in the Earth,
flay with club-like branches
as they bend and bow, billowing in the wind.
Leaves, carefree, falling furiously.
A paint palette of colour in their dance of death.

And through the darkness, I see into a homely house.
Brightly blazing, a fire flaming furiously.
A roaring spirit.
Hissing. Embers ending.
Chocolate child crouching by the logs
slurping at comfort in the cold of the night.
A dusty covering of frost
stealthily crawling, weaving a web across my face
as dazzling diamonds deck dull branches.

And the darkness of the night respectfully greets the day
as early morning mists mourn that the night has passed away.

Peter G T Schapira

November Day

Diamond strings on rose hip red,
Hang over leaves of autumn bed
The frost of hoar on rigid blades,
As the orb glows through,
and morning fades.
And through the mist of November land,
The fox will creep in copse of white,
by winter's hand.
He stirs companions into cold air
To fly and seek the berries there,
scattered far as autumn's store,
As hunger begs and calls once more.

The sloe with frost upon its skin
Hang high to show the blue within.
The hedgerow tall along our way,
Another feast from nature's haul.
Free for all, no debt to pay.
And as we pause and feel the cold,
We see the picture painted bold.
A scene of grey, of mist and haze,
This November day upon which we gaze.

Beneath our feet, the acorns crush,
We almost feel the seasons rush,
They leap and dance and pass us by,
As we see the joy of November sky

E C Hersey

FAREWELL

I am a leaf
Must decorate myself
Prepare;
For the journey ahead
For a farewell unique
And rare
Bridal yellow, red
Or burgundy brown
Delight my companion
With brightly coloured gown
Decorate my tree
With a departing gift
Of exorbitant beauty
Before sadness creeps in
With a heart heavy
And lonely
Devoid of all life
I must fall
Stand tall darling
Do not weep at all
Our fate allowed only
This much stay
The season has come
We must part our ways

Nayyar Ali Chandella

IDEAS OF WINTER

During his two year re-education Li Zhensheng photographs, as a
metaphor, grass piercing snow, to say: 'If winter is there, springtime
can only be round the corner'
Qing'an County, Li Zhensheng

Blanket white dunes:
Grass antennae stems pierce out,
Surreal,
Like thick tough hairs -
Only two -
On a very bald scalp.

Spring, a laughing wig
Sported
By the ageing earth.

Mike Loveday

GOLDEN LAND

The sunset makes a distant land,
Islands in the sky:
Bays and fingered isthmus -
- From different clouds on high
Mountains and rivers, to the shore:
A heavenly world, a paradise,
Lit gold in clear blue sky;
These islands of the blessed.
Now we have a hostile land,
As the sunset fades away;
The clouds have become the arctic,
With ice flows to the fore,
Confirmed, approved by
Flight of geese;
Reality once more.

John L Wigley

WINTRY WEATHER

Winter lightning
Western gales
Sullen winds cry,
Ice-cold storms
Wintry weather
Driving rain
Slanting sleet and snow.
Dying gales
A heavy hour
Black clouds billow
In midnight breeze.
Daybreak dawns
Unveiling the pale sun's
Lack of power.

Geoff Carnall

WINTER

Winter is cold,
And I am old,
Freezing fog,
Like a smog,
Only the warm,
Summer air,
Will keep my
Limbs in shape,
Winter is snow,
And frost,
Made for skiers,
And skaters,
Not for us,
Late comers.

B Brown

WINTER

Walking slowly through the snow
Trying not to fall
I see some happy children playing
And memories I recall
Snowballing and skating
I saw my youthful past
I thought then, that these long lost days
Would forever last
Now stopping just to get my breath
I heard a small boy cry
'Can you build a snowman?'
I said I'd give a try
And putting down my basket
I could not help but smile
I haven't built a snowman
For a long, long while
The snow went down my mittens
But still I wasn't cold
The years they simply slipped away
I was no longer old
Then putting in the final touch
We both did agree
The snowman was a work of art
For everyone to see
Then suddenly the boy had gone
He disappeared from sight
And the snowman seemed to wink his eye
Upon that winter's night

Pamela Popp

136

OVER TIME

Lead me down the leafy lane
Sun shining gently through the summer rain.
Take me into fields of grass so green,
Against the old oak tree, just let me lean.

Winding hedges along the dyke
Brings out in me the country tyke.
Birdsong and sounds from far and near
Rabbits run beneath the rutting deer.

I thought forever, it would last,
As a young boy far in the past.
My time was forever and a day
Asleep amongst the new mown hay.

And it seems now, without knowing,
My time on Earth is simply going.
Right from being a country boy
The countryside has given me so much joy.

Like everyone, I also know,
By God's hand, I will go.
And all the beauty that we find,
Sadly, we leave it all behind.

Dear God, I just want for you to see
What this countryside has meant to me.
So lay me beneath the grassy bank, alongside
the winding river.
And as it simply flows along, my soul can rest forever.

Jeff Hobson

WINTER

The worst winter in living memory
they say it was since 1947 -
when Fittie folk forded the frozen Dee.
As for us kids, we'd died and gone to Heaven,
snow white and crisp and even.

Thirty years later, we came home on leave
from Cairo, where Ra, the great sun god, rose
each dawn. At Levens Bridge, so some believe,
they sighted polar bears and Eskimos,
snow white and crisp and even.

The igloo we had rented just sufficed
to keep alive the feeble pulse of life.
Our noses, toes and fingertips were iced.
The searing wind chill stabbed us like a knife,
snow crisp and white and even.

We ventured out to buy fire-lighters, sticks,
bread for survival, milk and some hard tack.
The Ford Cortina stuck on the A6,
making it through to Carnforth but not back,
snow crisp and white and even.

One evening: *Rat-a-tat* upon the door -
Brian, from Egypt, in a wolfskin coat
that swathed him, cap-a-pié, from head to floor.
Flames licked, wine sang and laughter warmed the throat,
snow crisp and white and even.

Next day, our landlord in his Hyundai
invited us to help him toss some hay
out for the sheep. Under a turquoise sky,
Windermere seemed like paradise that day,
snow white and crisp and even.

Norman Bissett

The Sea Front In Winter

In the depths of winter, with all the tourists gone
Weathered beach huts sulking, dank, the weeks drag on.
Few, the local people, who braving wind and rain,
Watch the ocean's anger straining rope and chain.

Here a well wrapped grandma dragged from cake and tea,
Conned to take grandchildren out to view the sea.
Tossing rain-streaked pebbles at the hostile waves,
Trapped in childish revels, though her hearth she craves.

Anorak and scarf clad, hapless hound in tow
Canine slave and master make a sorry show.
Unlike stalwart granny, must keep pressing on
Windswept heads cast downwards, tacking up the prom.

Patient treasure hunter quartering the sands
Seeking artefacts mislaid by long forgotten hands.
Coins dropped by a Roman; axe head from a Dane.
Checking metal flotsam, ancient items perhaps to gain.

Lonely man in parka, facing waves of grey,
Standing on a groyne top, sheathed in icy spray.
Daydreams he's an admiral arousing naval pride,
Oblivious of weather and the restless running tide.

Sturdy souls, or foolish? Praise them or decry?
Few would wish to join them 'neath such sullen skies.
A hibernation aura on all there seems to be.
On hotels, pier, and kiosks, but not the restless sea.

Desolate the prom now, sand and pebble strewn
But this mask the sea front will discard quite soon.
Transformation dawning as stealthy time moves on
To banish dreary winter, with all the tourists gone.

Richard J Bradshaw

WINTER'S HERE

Shut the curtains, light the fire
It's very cold, winter's here
Icicles hang like metal spikes from the gutters
Beautiful patterns materialise on the frozen puddles
Snow hangs precariously from the trees
Silence all around
Snow falls, roads closed, schools shut
Sledging and snowball fights
Kids have fun
Danger lurks on frozen ponds
Drivers curse, slip and slide
Crash, bang, wallop!
Claim forms are in the post
Weather front is changing, rain is on the way
So all that fun and aggro
Will be gone for another day.

Teresa R Chester

I LOVE . . .

I love the winter,
So crisp, so bright,
I love to see the white snow fall at night.
I love to see the trees laid bare,
I love to see my warm breath in the air.
I love winter - to wrap up warm,
It's like the Earth has a rest - before a storm.
I love winter - it makes me smile,
I love to sit - and think for a while. . .

Helen Dakin

SHADOWS

How long the shadows lie along the grass,
And longer still when winter comes to pass.

The winds then blow so cold across the field
And all the walkers must to winter yield.

Wrapped to the nines in coats so warm,
No bitter wind can ever do them harm.

All praying for the year to turn once more
With growing warmth to melt them to the core.

And then it's summer clothes and boiling sun
With shadows shrinking further, every one.

Before we know it, round it goes again
Shadows lengthen. We wish for warmth in vain.

Katherine Warington

WINTER'S FIRST BLAST

First snow sits atop the midden
As I scrunch through the bitter chill
Friz to bone
As an icepool cracks 'neath my weight
Blue sky recedes before the clouds lowering in from the north
I puff steam in the air
As grass stands rigid to attention, unyielding before the bitter breeze
A raven contemptuously surveys my backyard
Where icicles drip
As I scurry back inside to my cup of tea and central heating
Defeating
Winter's first icy blast.

Maddoc Martin

IN THE BLEAK MIDSUMMER

In the bleak midsummer, technically
it should be warm, instead
I'm sat atop a windy moor, I'm riding out a storm.
My car is punished by each gust of wind,
told off for parking here, with
assumptions that the sun would shine,
the view, it would
be clear.

Mountain sheep, they know not what the month,
they're buffeted by debris, with
no memory sufficient to realise
what time of year it be.
My sunglasses in glove box stay
my side lights break the mist of day,
my fingers crossed that off the moor
the sky won't hold the clouds I saw.

Megan Davies

WINTER

An open book upon my lap, the music soft and low,
a crackling fire of burning logs gives off a warming glow.

The flickering shadows leap about the corners of the room,
the flames burst up and dissipate all vestiges of gloom.

I feel contentment deep within, it weaves a silken thread,
I hold this moment close to me, I will not let it ebb.

This winter's eve means more to me than long, hot summer nights,
or holidays with sun and sea spent drinking in the sights.

And so I sit and read my book and feel such utter bliss,
the smile upon my face spreads wide, evoked from life's sweet kiss.

Muriel Nicola Waldt

A Sign Of Winter

The cold wind whistles around the door,
A sign that winter is here once more,
Jack Frost at the window saying, 'I'm here to stay,'
A season of burst pipes could be on its way.

All the leaves of red and gold,
Have dropped from the trees, making them quite bald,
Animals hibernate, food is stored high,
They sense how much they need to survive and not die.

Wish I could forget that winter is here,
As it means all your fuel bills then get so dear,
You increase the heating, increase the light,
I think I'll hibernate, it sounds just right.

It seems such a never-ending night,
As during the day there's so little light,
In the garden, bulbs are planted year after year,
And you know that winter's over when flowers reappear.

Barbara Holme

Winter Den

the robin heralds
the winters here
he pecks upon
my window clear
he feeds from the nuts
upon the tree
and chirps his song
merrily
robin redbreast
come again
and brighten up
my winter den.

Margery Rayson

WINTER

Winter is the mourning season,
For the summers that have passed,
The season of interment
For the thoughts that should ne'er be cast.

Winter is the weeping season,
For those who have lost all faith,
Haunting with its mists and chills
The restless spirit of the wraith.

Winter is the healing season,
For the wounds that run so deep,
A place of solitary reflection
On what dreams we need to keep.

Winter is the contemplating season,
For the time we have yet to live,
Endless hours of constant questions
On what we have to give.

Winter is the shifting season,
That sees a new age dawn,
A place where rivers of notions run
And the seeds of hope are born.

Malcolm Dewhirst

WINTER WHITE

Like tinsel on a Christmas tree
That burns brightly in the night,
Fine lacework on the spider webs,
Sparkling strings of light.

At dawn the park is fairyland,
Alive with a silvery glow.
At first the frost, with diamonds
Then the crystalline snow.

The green of open common
Becomes a white world overnight.
Disguised by the elfin artist,
Who shuns the colours bright.

With palette very limited,
Delicate is his touch.
With just a dash of robin red,
A little, not too much.

Flakes of snow in pristine shower,
Making magic every night.
With mystic brush, feathered quill,
The world is winter white.

Patricia Adele Draper

SHIVERING THOUGHTS

I've never been a winter lover
can't stand the cold at all,
give me the spring or summer
or even early fall.
Don't wish to be a meanie
but snow I'd happily ban,
as I can't see the point of it
It's meaningless to man,
What does it do but make you shiver
brings colds and flu galore,
breaks our limbs when ices up
freezing nature's pretty floor.

Winter wonderland you say
with the trees all looking bare,
ponds all frozen, poor little ducks
the birds have gone elsewhere.
Nature's lost its happy smile
Its colours dull and grey,
our flowers and plants no longer grow
too cold for them to stay.
So what is this wonder may I ask
this winter that's cruel and bland,
that takes away the beauty
of a wonderful, colourful land.

Brenda Birchall

WINTER

The snow falls nicely,
The frost lies icily.

The fog thickens vastly,
The thunder clashes nastily.

Christmas is very near,
Santa Claus will travel here.

Darkness arrives early,
Pleased it is only yearly.

Cold and flu spreads far and wide,
Making people stay inside.

Houses have their heating on,
The cold affects everyone.

This season is the worst,
With clouds of snow that soon will burst.

But do not despair, as you will see,
Spring will be here, believe you me.

Throughout this season of cold and wet,
Be happy and jolly and do not fret.

Gordon Collinson

SEASONAL AFFECTIVE DISORDER

There's clouds on far horizons
Squalls upon the sea
The darkness is descending
Winter's not for me

Depressing, gloomy nights and days
A time for contemplation
Happiness dies as time turns back
That's my honest observation

The only worthy consolation
The pub is nice and warm
A jug of ale brings solace
In any shape or form

Bring on summer sunshine
Let this murky sky turn blue!
In times of celebration
I rarely think of you

There is an answer to my plight
I'm considering emigration
Spain or Greece or Portugal
It's a serious temptation

John Robinson

AUTUMN'S END

Love, the afternoon comes fast. I cannot
Face it. The fading light too
Quick. My hands stick
the paper blank, no words
spill from my pen. It is
gummed up with sorrow, stuck
in yesterday. Today speaks of
loneliness; the doctor's orders
do not work. Not on this day.
Today, Love, I am left
to other devices, the broken
promise, still in my hand
pale and lifeless.
I cannot mend it; sew these
bits together. Help, come
home soon, before the dying
of the light. Before I am sucked
with the tide, that pulls hard
and fast at my ankles. I am
helpless to the horizon,
A lost and hungry ghost.
I want nothing but the light.
Light and your love.

Sadi Ranson-Polizzotti

SEVEN THIRTY

Vapour trails across the sky
Pink thread on silk of blue
Birds singing, flying, fluttering
In the dawn so new

Cold, white frost lies on the grass
So still the morning air
Trees silhouette against the sun
Stripped of dress, so bare

Breath billows out like chimney smoke
Feet and hands so cold
Marching bravely through the thicket
Stick grasped with firm hold

Frightened rabbits run for cover
Deer startled to a halt
Pheasants head for trees and bushes
Cows stand still, prepared to bolt

Further on the stream lies frozen
Not a trickle to be heard
Just the tapping on the surface
The break of a thirsty bird

Turning round, the sun is higher
Warmer walking home this way
Toes and finger snuggled cosy
And the promise of a beautiful day

Christine M J Oatley

WINTER BLUES

The sky is getting darker as the sun creeps off to bed
leaving the moon to patrol the skies and the night that lies ahead
Squirrels are busy gathering berries and nuts galore
darting here, dashing there, frantically searching everywhere
filling up their store

the trees dismiss the leaves and throw them to the ground
where they lay like fallen soldiers, not making any sound
The wind turns harsh and angry and races through the sky
uplifting plants, hurling litter, gaining pace and growing bitter
as people rush on by

The park looks sparse and empty where once young children played
the atmosphere is cold and damp, where once the sunlight laid
Everyone has ventured home and shut themselves away
from bitter winds, falling snow, to sit by fires all aglow
to mourn the fading day

Bright stars appear like magic, putting on a show
then one by one street lamps light up to halt the moonlight glow
But the moonlight sky is stronger and commands the night to fall
growing darker, looking black, night moves in, no turning back
no sunlight left at all

I sit and watch in wonder as the season hatches out
to leave us with pure beauty, of that there is no doubt
The ever changing colours and the warmth that they will bring
So go fly a kite, splash in the rain, enjoy the season and take the gain
for soon it will be spring!

Wendy Orlando

Another Wintry Day

Summer's light has gone,
Winter's light God turned on.
Against the red, frigid early morning sky,
A flock of birds silhouetted, fly by.
Their black outline of their shapes,
White frost over the house is draped.
Another wintry day start
With the crank of a motor car,
Forgot the de-icer ah?
On the radio, weather warning,
for later this morning,
Transcendental rain forecast,
Into the evening last.
Nothing about this winter pleasing.
Put another log on the fire,
So the flames burn higher.

George B Clarke

The Wonder Of Winter

Silently, softly the snowflakes are falling
The drab, dreary day painted silvery white,
Magical moments have turned the grim greyness
To a fantasy world filled with sparkling light.

Glum, gloomy children are suddenly smiling
As feathery flakes fall from the wintry sky.
'Where are the woolly hats, where are the wellies,
The mittens and mufflers? Come quickly,' they cry.

They rush from the room in a whirlwind of madness,
Soon cheeks are rosy and eyes sparkling bright
For there's so much to do in this wonderful weather
When the wonder of winter turns a grey day to white.

Barbara Dunning

CHANGING TIMES

Your leaves turn from green, to orange and red
The wind blows cold and the summer comes to an end
The squirrel collects nuts and in your branches makes his bed
And as winter takes hold, the gales make your body bend

Then soon those beautiful leaves begin to fall
They lie like a multicoloured carpet around your base
Your body at last bare, looks so slender and tall
The leaves crumble to dust and blow away without a trace

You wait patiently through the winter time
Quietly standing through rain, wind and snow
You know shortly there will come a sign
When the birds begin to sing and the sun again will glow

Then one day tiny buds appear
Small, green leaves along your branches grey and worn
You know at last that spring is here
And once again you'll take your majestic form.

Gail Wooton

WINTER TALES

As we sit, the firelight flickers.
Friendly shadows on the wall
Whisper softly autumn's over,
Summer is beyond recall.
Snowy mantles soon will cover
Every inch of brown and green.
Jaunty robin will delight us
Whenever he comes on the scene.
Winter chill may wreak much havoc
With icy roads and blustery gales
Yet long, dark nights we'll fill with pleasure
As we recount our winter tales.

Rosemary Thomson

JANUARY SNOW

January snow:
It creeps upon us silently in the night
Soundlessly laying over the land
Like a soft, white blanket,
Covering, quietening everything.

As morning first awakes, the snow is perfect,
Crisp, clean, pure, white, silent, still.
The world seems to have slowed,
Quiet and in slow motion.

The branches hang heavy on the trees.
Everything looks the same.
Where does the grass end and the path begin?
Only the snow knows.

Fresh untrodden snow, undisturbed and unspoiled,
As I walk on it, I leave my deep footprints.
Can I hear the soft crunch underfoot
Or can I only feel it?

The red streaked sky issues its traditional warning:
Another cold, clear, beautiful day of January snow.

Matt Ebeling

SNOW

Where is my mother today?
Hiding in the folds of this frozen ice-queen.
This double-edged sword, that glitters under silver moon.

Plough on!

Frustration forms in the foothills,
of this frozen fairyland.
Broken blisters bleeding,
into brand new boots.
Swearing, sinking, sliding,
off the road again.
Children running, returning,
chapped hands raw, burning.

Plough on!

Oh! Bring back the blessed sun!
Fix this faulty furnace.
Season of sickness.
Let me warm my wounds
against the blossoming bosom
of Mother Earth
again . . .

Tracey Rosehorse

EAST ANGLIA
(January 2003)

Off northern seas the arctic blasts
Blow virgin snow to Norfolk soil
A freezing blanket - frosty nights
And bitter winds to make it raw

In '53 saw tragic floods
From Lincolnshire along the coast
Many drowned and homes were lost
Could it happen here again?

Thus onwards 50 years this week
Chaotic scenes with stranded cars
The M11 could not cope
With icy lanes in Cambridgeshire.

Soon there'll be some milder days
Come February with snowdrops gay
And into March with spring in step
To greet the darling buds of May.

Steve Glason

AND WINTER WAITS

January brilliance drives natural lines
to clear sky - but for a fragment cloud -
furrows to darken fields -
condenses oaks to brown badges -
hedges to blackest bands.

The world outside is windscreen real.
But we stay - artificial -
locked inside our engine's summer warmth -
pass by the scene
compelled in our denial of planetary force.

And winter waits.

Sue Britchford

INFORMATION

We hope you have enjoyed reading this book - and that you will continue to enjoy it in the coming years.

If you like reading and writing poetry drop us a line, or give us a call, and we'll send you a free information pack.

Alternatively if you would like to order further copies of this book or any of our other titles, then please give us a call or log onto our website at www.forwardpress.co.uk

Anchor Books Information
Remus House
Coltsfoot Drive
Peterborough
PE2 9JX
(01733) 898102